EXPENSE
— TO —
PROFIT

To my best friend, my wife, Sheri.
She is my cheerleader,
providing constant support,
guidance, and unwavering inspiration.

My son, Max, who expertly partners with me in expense reduction.
My daughter, Hallie, and son-in-law, Vlad,
and granddaughters, Lily and Mia, who add lots of zest to life.

To my parents, siblings and their spouses, and my in-laws who are
always willing to provide advice, support, and be there.

Publishing and Design:

EP♦C AUTHOR
P U B L I S H I N G

Ordering Information: Special discounts are available on quantity purchases. For details contact us below.

Please contact: 240-406-9075 | marc@expensetoprofit.com | expensetoprofit.com

First Edition

EX/PENSE

— TO —

PROFIT

ELIMINATE THE COSTS THAT SABOTAGE YOUR GROWTH

— MARC FREEDMAN —

What Others Are Saying About Expense To Profit

When we hired you and told you under no circumstances were we changing our banking relationship, you said, "That was fine." I was truly surprised because I thought the only way we would save money was to change banking institutions. When you reviewed our fees and provided your analysis showing us that we were overpaying by $32,000 in the last year, I was flabbergasted. Our banker had told us that this is the best he could do. I approached him after our meeting, and they offered to reduce our fees by $9,000.

When I reported back to you the bank's proposal, and they argued that our assessment was not correct, you then provided us with the information to show them that they were not charging the market rates for the relationship like we had with them. Armed with that data, they reduced our fees that provided savings to almost $30,000 per year. Still surprised but could not have accomplished this without your assistance.

—**Client since 2014**, CFO, dental practice
Milwaukee, WI

We were referred to Expense To Profit through an adviser we are using. When Marc reviewed our expenses, he noticed we had not claimed any R&D Tax Credits. We are not sure why our existing CPA never suggested we file for those credits. Marc and his CPA R&D Tax Credit team found we did qualify and also provided the forms necessary to amend our past three years of returns to recover the overpaid taxes. In addition, he and his team will also support us should the IRS have any inquiries regarding our amended returns for no additional fee.

—**Client since 2018**, CEO, *robotics company*
East Peoria, IL

When ETP talked to us about reducing our food and produce spend, I didn't think there would be much room for improvement, especially, as they said without sacrificing quality or service levels. The results were surprising for a few reasons. First, they considered that pricing was not our only consideration, and their recommendations were based on product quality, vendor service, and pricing. Their analysis showed our spending could be reduced by 18.5% for our non-center of the plate expenses, and 9.4% from our existing produce vendor.

During the first two months, our savings exceeded their estimates, and we are impressed with the vendor, who is excellent to work with. Having ETP perform the analysis, execute the decisions we made, and their continued monitoring of our invoices freed up not only money but the time to set and focus on other priorities. Between the information, insight, and time and money saved, the project was very successful.

—**Client since 2016**, General Manager/COO, *country club*
Fairfax, VA

Marc reviewed our Payroll and HR services and showed us how combining them to a single provider would be helpful in reducing redundancies and provide a cost savings as well. He brought in three providers for us to interview to determine the best fit for us. He and his team negotiated the services and pricing and cut our costs by 42% over our current provider. It has been six months since the change, and we could not be happier. Our onboarding, time and attendance, and employee information are all located on one platform. The transition to the new provider was almost seamless. They provided the training and a team dedicated to making sure our transition was successful. Not sure if we could have made this decision and completed the implementation on our own. Marc is an invaluable resource.

—**Client since 2017**, CFO, country club
Arlington, VA

After Expense To Profit was successful in other expense areas, we discussed doing a health insurance benefits review. We had just received our annual renewal and were surprised that the costs were only going to be 2.5% higher. They contacted our current provider and actually secured a reduction of 7% from the prior year.

While negotiating with our current carrier, they surveyed the marketplace for additional providers we might want to consider. Their analysis provided additional savings of 10% (total 22.5% from the original renewal offer) and a better plan for our company. More surprising is this was done while keeping all deductibles and annual limits the same and providing more benefits. Our employees and their families thank you!

—**Client since 2015**, HR Director, biotechnology company
Rockville, MD

We hired Expense To Profit as they suggested they could find savings even though we were currently purchasing thru a GPO. I was sure that we had the best pricing as our procurement group is very diligent in negotiating our purchases. While the process took a bit longer than they originally thought, as it was a complex RFP process, the results were worth the wait. They found savings of over $650,000 for us that we can now deploy elsewhere. Most importantly, they provide us a monthly report that shows each item purchased vs. the baseline that was originally created, showing we are, in fact, receiving the savings.

—**Client since 2016**, CEO, multi-discipline medical group
Rye, NY

As a non-profit, every dollar in costs takes from the services we are able to provide in fulfilling our mission. When we hired you, we were skeptical that you would find any savings. We had recently switched to a new provider because they provided 20% savings above the previous merchant processing company. Because we had just made a change, I had told you I was reluctant to make a change as it is so disruptive.

Your analysis found that we were not on the correct code for the payment types we were receiving. I was shocked as we just changed providers six months earlier and could not believe that two different companies in this business missed that. I believe it was because when you interviewed us, we answered questions that had never been asked by any providers in the past. This classification change provides over $100,000 in savings per year that we no longer need to fundraise for. Thank you so much—what a valuable service you provide and are looking forward to seeing what else you can find.

—**Client since 2017**, Executive Director, non-profit organization
Washington, DC

Marc and his team reviewed our workers' compensation insurance policy. When he asked if we had ever done a claims audit, I replied, "I was not sure, but we monitor our claims monthly and our agent takes care of that for us." After receiving our claims history, they found eight claims that were not closed properly and two that were never closed.

When they went back to our carrier and reviewed each claim, they were able to get all of the claims corrected and closed properly. I was not aware that if you have been overcharged premiums, you need to request a refund, or the carrier can keep those overpaid premiums. In addition to getting back over $100,000 in overpaid premiums, our MOD rate was reduced, causing a lower renewal rate for the current year. Thank you, what a valuable service.

—**Client since 2013**, President, janitorial cleaning services
Washington, DC Metro

We hired Expense To Profit to review multiple expense categories. We had negotiated new pricing for all of our offices 12 months earlier, saving 20% with a major office supply company. They reviewed what we were buying, and I was shocked to learn they would save us an additional 18%.

We are six months in, and they have delivered, and the reports they provide are invaluable. Additionally, they set up a list of the most commonly purchased supplies which all office managers purchase from daily. They can still purchase off that list but needs management approval. This has eliminated a lot of the rogue purchasing that used to occur.

—**Client since 2013**, CFO, multi-office medical practice
Washington, DC

We have a lot of software solutions that we use in our firm. More importantly, we had no idea which users were actually using the different solutions we pay for every month. Marc showed us a solution that discovers all your SaaS subscriptions and identifies any unused, underused, or abandoned licenses.

Once installed, we were able to discover, manage, and optimize our firm's SaaS subscriptions and licenses to reduce "shadow SaaS," manage renewals, reduce our spend and secure user accounts. Our IT department insisted doing this was a waste of money; however, the ROI was five months, and the management of this expense is now under control.

—**Client since 2017**, CEO, multi-office law firm
USA

When we interviewed Marc and his team, we were sure they would not be able to help as we went to the market daily to get best pricing for our shipments. We spent over 5 hours daily calling our menu of up to 15 companies. Once Expense To Profit finished their review, they determined we could cut that list of 15 to 4 or 5 trucking companies.

They created a matrix based on shipping lanes of who to use and automated the process. We were able to redeploy that employee to a different part of the company where he could be more useful. The result is we are saving 27% over prior years, which is almost $350,000 annually. With the cost of vanilla beans doubling in the past year, this helps our current cash flow.

—**Client since 2016**, CFO, vanilla manufacturer
Waukegan, IL

Our relationship with Expense To Profit is a true partnership. They have introduced us to solution providers that truly think "outside the box." As a smaller consulting practice, it is always challenging to compete with your larger competitors. Marc and his team have found ways to make that a reality. We are now able to afford to offer benefits that are almost identical to our larger competitors. The monthly reports provided always have new insights into additional solutions we should consider. We thank you as does our entire team of employees and their families.

—**Client since 2012**, Managing Partner
professional consulting group
Washington, DC

Marc and his team of experts found that we were overpaying our telecom and data services vendor by 24%. During his analysis, he discovered we were paying for phone lines that were not even in service and recovered those overpaid costs going back three years, I was not aware you could do that, but he was and got us a full credit.

The even better part was Expense To Profit did this without changing providers. I was sure he was telling me a story and selling me a line when he said that they have pricing information that if I asked my business representative would say to you did not exist. Apparently, it does really exist. Thanks for helping us be more successful! I can use the found money for business development and grow my business.

—**Client since 2011**, President, marketing solutions company
New York, NY

Expense To Profit was able to reduce our energy supply costs by 18%. When you consume over 1 million megawatts annually, that is significant savings that we were able to pass on to our tenants. We have renewed our rate a second time now, and he was able to keep the increase to only 2% even though the supply markets are substantially higher than they were three years ago.

—**Client since 2015**, VP, property management
Libertyville, IL

You reviewed our contract and found that we were paying 50% more than other providers charge for identical services. When you approached our current provider, they told you that they would not renegotiate the contract, and it is "buyer beware." Really, they have been servicing our building for 15 years, and that was their reply. We terminated our agreement with them, paid the termination fee, and will still save 41% over the next three years with our new vendor.

—**Client since 2017**, building owner
McLean, VA

TABLE OF CONTENTS

Why Tackle Expense Reduction?

I f you have owned a business for any length of time, you know that it comes with the freedom to run things YOUR way and on YOUR time.

However, in the quest for that freedom, many business owners are focused almost exclusively on generating revenue. Most would say that without fresh revenue coming into the business, the business fails.

Revenue is certainly important, but if that revenue is overtaken by the added expense of adding that revenue, it defeats the purpose of generating that revenue in the first place. If you create $1 million in new money in a year but it costs you $2 million to produce it, you're operating at a net loss.

That's not sustainable in the long run.

In the quest to be profitable, there are also businesses that focus on reducing costs. While that's not a bad idea, they often do so at the expense of those activities that, in fact, generate the revenue in the first place.

When businesses hit a difficult patch, they might concentrate on reducing advertising expenses or cutting staff. If advertising is bringing in the qualified leads that you need, or if the staff you are cutting generates needed revenue, it's a counterproductive move at best.

The correct answer is to reduce expenses *without* changing anything that you are currently doing.

If this is your goal, then you are in the right place.

I've helped companies successfully reduce their expenses for over 35 years, and over 89% of our clients have not had a need to change vendors or suppliers at any point in this process.

Because we are familiar with nearly every industry out there and have a working knowledge of the pricing that can be obtained, we find great success in helping our clients save a lot of money on things they are already spending it on.

Save without having to cut back on revenue-generating activities AND without cutting staff.

You're probably wondering how we do that.

In this book, we will go into detail and the processes we use, exploring case studies across various industries where what we do actually *works*.

As you read through this, you will probably find examples that resonate with you and your current situation.

Many people take the do-it-yourself approach to expense reduction. We've encountered many clients who started by trying it on their own first. Then were amazed when they reached out to us and got results that they themselves weren't able to get.

So…who is this book for?

This book is for three different segments of the marketplace:

➢ An entrepreneur who's trying to get their business up and running, someone who is in the $1 million to $10 million revenue range.

➢ The business that is in a growth and scaling phase, which is at $10 million to $100 million in revenues.

➢ Those companies that are hitting their stride, at the $100 million plus levels.

We find that these are the segments that benefit from these strategies the most because they are big enough to benefit from the methods we employ when working with them. They already have the scale and leverage that allow us to best utilize the relationship we already have with the same vendors and suppliers they are using.

We find that our clients come to us because most of these businesses are stuck. They're stuck because of their success, and they don't have the cash flow that they need to be able to take the business to the next level.

And in addition to that, not having that cash flow they need, they're paying for things at rates that are probably not what we would consider market prices.

The different solutions that we bring to the table, in addition to business practices, are actually "spending practices."

Most consultants don't do what we do. They don't spend time on spending habits. In their attempt to get the "best" prices they think are available, a lot of businesses will do RFXs, which are requests for quotes, requests for information, or requests for proposal.

But that's old school, and you're not necessarily getting the best price.

Because of that, we've got different strategies that we use and deploy for our clients with direct negotiations with vendors. If we can't be successful with direct negotiations, then the next approach is to utilize a reverse auction process to get market prices.

Reverse auctions?

This a fun and interesting strategy, but to learn what it is, you'll need to keep reading.

I will be describing this and many more approaches in detail, and as I mentioned, an abundance of case studies to illustrate the results of these methods.

If this has intrigued you so far, I'm about to open up a whole new world for you, because as the old saying goes, "You don't know what you don't know."

Let's dive in and eliminate costs that sabotage your business!

Increased freedom and profitability are on the horizon.

MARC FREEDMAN, CEO, CERC
Certified Expense Reduction Consultant
Helping you spend money smarter

E**X**PENSE
— TO —
PROFIT

CHAPTER 1

Is Your Business Failing to Live Up to Its Financial Potential?

As I mentioned in the opening, *we don't always know what we don't know*. Many businesses move through their day thinking that everything is fine, not knowing they have financial problems that could be easily solved. Other companies know full well they have issues that need to be addressed.

However, the solutions either choose to implement are simply Band-Aids and not long-term answers to their challenges.

In order for us to fully assist a company, we address the need to look deep into the solution.

After all, if a company like ours can help your business find money that it didn't even know it had, wouldn't you want to know about it?

A perfect example of how we do this happened with a client in 2020.

This owner has a big electrical business. He was doing $25 million a year until COVID-19 hit, but then his revenues are down about 25%.

It's been a family business for 63 years. The father and brother started it, and then passed it to the two sons. The two sons are now ready to explore getting out of the business.

We were brought in to review how they're doing and what they're doing. Our goal was to discover, first of all, whether or not they were operating with best practices. We found out very quickly on our phone call that they were not.

As we started having conversations with them, we began to tick down the different expense line items. I found it very interesting because he's old school in his processes. Part of his business is old school, and the rest of his business has actually moved more into the current century.

During our conversation, they said, "We've had this **accounting package** that's for the electrical repair business industry for about 30 years."

Not surprised by this admission, I said, "And you really found no need or didn't want to upgrade that while you've been upgrading everything else?"

He responded, "Oh no, we have the top of the line stuff there. But the accounting part's not."

I asked, "So, how do you know you're spending what you're supposed to spend?"

He said, "I don't...but I also have a leasing company, so I **lease vehicles** back to this business. And then we brought in Enterprise, and it's amazing that they can charge less than I charge."

I told him, "Well, there are probably two reasons for that. Number one, you have created your own program, which is great, and second, their costs for maintenance are substantially less than your costs because they're doing a lot of cars all the time."

"Oh, I didn't look at it that way. I just figured because I could charge more, I did. But I don't really make any money out of it."

So, I asked, "Why do you do it then?"

"Because I've always done it that way."

That statement is often the death of all progress, isn't it? As our discussion continued, he also mentioned that he had hired someone to make sure he wasn't overpaying on his real estate taxes, and he was sure that was the right solution.

I asked if he had ever done a **cost segregation analysis** with his accountant. Like most people, he wasn't clear about what that meant.

Then I asked, "Well, have you ever had to do updates to the building? If the building is as old as you said it is, you've had to at some point, right?"

He had done a few updates.

"And how did you handle this?"

"Well, they're on the, you know, they're on the, um ..." He had no idea what to call it, but he was referring to the sheet that you file with the federal government where you depreciate the value of property over time.

I said, "The rules changed years ago, and you can take all those federal depreciations that have been there forever and accelerate it to today. Did you know that?"

"I can?"

"Yeah."

He replied, "But that's not going to help the business."

I said, "No, it won't because you own the property, BUT you'll get a dollar for dollar tax credit for all of those items."

"Me, personally?"

"Yeah."

He realized that he's going to have a big windfall he had no idea he could have. So, the problem is that a lot of businesses don't pay attention until something dramatic happens in the marketplace that affects them personally.

Of course, the pandemic has affected a lot of different businesses. Many businesses always spent money because they had money to spend. They didn't necessarily pay attention to what things cost and whether or not they were really spending their money the right way.

Our ability to come in and reduce their expenses is really positive because every $1 in reduction of expenses is worth $3 to maybe $8 when one sells the business depending on the industry.

These guys have a goal of selling their company someday, so the better their profit and loss (P&L) is at the time of sale, the better the price they will get for it.

If we can drop their expenses by $1 million, that could effectively be somewhere between $3 million and $8 million more for them on the sale of the business. Clearly, the long-run payoff for implementing our process far outweighs the payout for our services.

This is a perfect illustration of how we launch our in-depth process regarding the questions we ask when we talk with clients, to find out, "How do you do it?"

If you have been spending your money in a particular way, are you willing to accept possibly doing it another way that will benefit you from a profitability standpoint?

If profit is important to your company—and it needs to be— why would business owners resist this?

One reason, as I just mentioned, is that people have no idea they need help. They've always done business in their particular way.

Let's explore some other key reasons...

Ego is the Biggest Killer of Progress

When we talk to business owners, the CEO, the chairman, the president, the executive director, or whoever that person is, they're always willing to make changes to make things better because it doesn't really involve them.

They're not the ones in the trenches making those changes. They're not the ones that have to implement those changes. However, they are about to learn that our process implements those changes FOR the business, and it makes things **a lot simpler.**

When we start talking about banks, for example, the person we are speaking with says, "Well, hold on, I'm not changing my bank." I say, "That's good, because over 99% of the time we don't change banks."

The person is very relieved.

Our goal is not to come in and upset the apple cart. Our goal is NOT to make vendor changes. That's why 89% of the time or more, depending on the expense category such as **bank or merchant fees,** we never change the vendors unless the existing vendor is not willing to acquiesce to what we found they were overcharging.

Consequently, our aim is to make sure that the client is comfortable with our process regarding how we find things. We do everything off site, so we have very little interaction with their staff to not interfere with the time crunch that most businesses are under.

Even in spite of this, some businesses will delay taking a good long look at how they are operating because they don't see that there is a problem.

Here's a perfect example of someone who didn't think they needed us when, in fact, they really did.

A good friend of mine manages small shopping plazas for a lot of real estate owners in my area. And he said, "I do all the real estate for a major pizza chain in the Washington, DC region. One guy owns all the franchises and all the locations; I ought to introduce you to him."

I agreed, so my friend introduces me to this guy. Three minutes into the conversation, he said, "Yeah, I don't need your services." I asked, "Really? How could you determine that so fast?" He told me, "I am the number one franchisee in the country."

I asked, "Oh, well you know, have you ever thought about this…?"

"Yeah, but that doesn't work."

"Did you try it?"

"No, why would we?"

So, I mentioned to him a couple of other things but his ego stepped in. I said, "You know, we've done some **workman's comp recoveries** and **premium reductions** for other franchisees in your system."

"You have?"

"We have."

"Yeah, but I'm sure my workman's comp rates are fine."

I told him, "You know, that's the same thing that we were told when we interacted with the number two franchisee in the country who, as you know, is in California. Why don't you call him and ask him how he enjoys that six-figure check he just received as a premium rebate because he was overcharged from his insurance company? Additionally, he will also enjoy an 8% reduction in premiums going forward."

Dead silence.

"Yeah, well, I don't need your services; I am the number one franchise in the system."

I said, "You know, I think they measured the number one ranking by revenue, not by profitability, but have a good day."

And I hung up the phone.

A lot of times ego gets in the way of what we're trying to help people do.

Don't ask a question you don't already know what the answer is expected to be. That's how I do my business, and that's why I responded to this individual the way I did. I already knew the answer.

Being involved in the business world for 40 years, specializing in just the expense side for the past ten years ... I'm not reinventing the wheel.

Gaining a good understanding of our client and what they are trying to do is critical. I'm here to solve the client's problems, not mine. Referring back to the electrical contractor, he and his cousin benefited from our services and are now ready to sell the business at some point in the near future.

We Tried It and It Didn't Work

When someone tells me that they've tried something and it didn't work, it doesn't always mean that it didn't work.

Trying something the wrong way and failing doesn't mean it can't work—it only means that your previous way failed. If Thomas Edison decided that the light bulb couldn't be invented after failing *once*, we would all be sitting in the dark.

Other times, we try something without having all of the information or expertise that we really needed.

One potential client shared with me that they "tried" what I was proposing and it "didn't work." After some questioning, he said he looked into making some changes five years ago.

A lot can change in five years.

He said he looked into changing his **payroll service** and when he finished his research, he realized that reducing his fees from $10,000 to $9,000 wasn't worth the hassle of changing vendors and working with someone he didn't know. He felt like it wasn't worth the bother.

After finding that out, I asked him, "Which check do you hate writing each month?"

I always ask that question because there is going to be some expense they need to pay, but typically they would rather not.

In my experience, nine out of ten times it seems to be a **health insurance or other benefit-related expense**, which is an area where we can be extremely helpful. Sure enough, that prospect responded as expected.

We've gone into businesses where their insurance agent has told them they have the best plan. They are told there are no more reductions that can be done unless you want to offload something to employees.

We get involved. We tell them we're not going to offload anything to employees, but let's review which employees are using what you're offering and what the level of consumption is for those plans.

We worked with a government contractor client, their insurance agent, and finished their enrollment. They were spending a $1.5 million a year on health insurance for their employees.

We looked at the plan and the usage of the plan. We found that they had a Cadillac option, the most expensive plan available, but nobody was enrolled in it. Well, that Cadillac option increased the premium by $150,000 a year. So instead of spending $1.5 million this next year, they'll spend $1,350,000 and all we did was remove an option that nobody was using.

I asked why they were offering this plan.

"Well, we just felt it was important to have something that somebody could use if they wanted to."

"Okay, how long have you had this plan?"

"Five years."

16

"So, nobody used it for the last two that we see. Anybody use it before then?"

"Don't think so."

I said, "If we're getting rid of something that nobody's using, nobody's going to know that we really got rid of it."

"Yeah, I guess that's right."

Then I said, "We could offer three new plans instead of the three that you have: the low-end like you currently have, the high-end that everybody's using, and something in between. Maybe we can even save you more money. And now, they'll see that they're in the highest plan instead of being in the middle plan."

He said, "Oh, that's an interesting concept."

"Think logically about how that works from an employee standpoint. They were in a medium plan and there was a higher plan that they couldn't afford. Now, they're in the highest plan and they can afford it. How does that make you feel as an employee? It's emotionally uplifting. And if you think about it in that light, that's a huge benefit to your employee base."

"Wow, never thought about that."

Then I told him, "Oh, and by the way, you can either leave the premiums where they are for the employee, or because we just reduced your cost by 10%, you can reduce their premiums by 10%. And you're going to pay less than you were paying before. Which way should we do it? It's your call."

Employees were going to now potentially save $100 a month on the "perceived" premium plan, and $20 a month on the non-premium plan. That's important.

The client opted to pass that savings on to their employees. The company was now paying less, so they wanted their team to enjoy the savings.

Imagine being able to tell your employees that they can keep their same insurance plan *and* pay less for it? That makes you a big hero and it's a huge morale booster.

What we do is help our clients look better.

Our entire purpose is to make your processes more efficient using strategies that everybody else is using, but maybe you hadn't deployed yet in your business.

Lack Of Buy-In from the Executive Team

Our goal, of course, is to work with the CEO or owner because that person is ultimately in charge of the final decision. However, they usually defer to their CFO, bookkeeper, or controller: aka the person in charge of the money.

I know how this usually goes, so I explain, "No, if I talk to them, they're either going to tell me that we need to schedule an appointment that they will break into two, three, four times. I'll call you in a month and tell you that we still haven't spoken."

"No, no, if I tell them, that's never going to happen."

"Okay."

I was calling on a mortgage company, and one of the partners, who was the chairman, said, "I'll have my CFO talk to you."

I called the CFO multiple times, and he didn't respond. I sent emails, still no response. A month went by, so I called the chairman as I promised. And updated him, "Your CFO, Dave, has never responded."

"What? I told him to reach out to you."

"Yeah, I know. But I told you this was going to happen." The partner couldn't believe it. But the reality is, this happens all the time.

Two weeks after that conversation, I still hadn't heard from Dave. So, we're now six weeks into it.

A week later, I attended a lunch with one of my network groups. A gentleman who was invited to that meeting as a visitor sat down next to me. He was one of the other partners in that mortgage company.

I knew who he was because I had seen his picture on their website as the president. I hadn't gotten anywhere with the chairman, so I thought this would be a great opportunity.

He said, "I know your name from somewhere, I can't place it."

"You know, Craig, I talked to your partner Brian, and he thought I should talk to Dave and Dave just hasn't responded. But I think I can help you based on conversations I had with Brian six weeks ago."

Craig said, "Hmm, I find that interesting."

That afternoon after the meeting, I got a phone call from Dave.

And I had a meeting with Dave two days later.

We went on to save them a lot of money.

Now why did Dave not call me back earlier? This happens a lot, as I mentioned. He could have been legitimately busy...or... he was afraid that I might find something, and he could have felt threatened by it—even to the point of potentially losing his job. Crucial to our professional working relationship, is to realize:

We're a partner with our clients, we aren't here to make anyone look bad.

We endeavor to help you look better because you and I are going to have a talk about how to take what you're doing today and tweak it just a little bit to make it cost less and have better results.

In that way, instead of looking at us as a threat, look at us as a partner. When this is understand, things can go very smoothly, and we can generate RESULTS for clients.

Finding that strong reason "why" is so important.

With our electrical contractor client, they were very motivated to reduce expenses and increase profits because the long-term plan was to sell their business for a higher valuation. For every dollar we saved them, they got three or more dollars back.

Wouldn't you do that? Of course, it's a no-brainer.

I am constantly looking for different opportunities that better enhance our client's bottom line, so my solutions are always evolving. Helping businesses reach their potential means I am continuously learning even though I have been at this for a long time.

For instance, let's talk about reimbursements from AP services.

There are providers out there that will pay bills for you using a **virtual debit card**, where the revenue comes back to the business based on what was charged on the card. So, if you think about a credit card, typically it has 2.5% to 3% fees. Maybe about 1% of that comes back to the business.

Some providers give less, but it is NEW revenue you never had previously.

I'm always looking for the provider that's not only going to satisfy the client's needs because it has to be a good fit, but also the service provider that's going to provide the best results for the client.

It's always good to have several providers to compare in the same industry, which we do, because every client is different, and every situation is different. No two are really alike.

Our goal is to match the best solution AND the best fit for each client.

Keep in mind, what we do is a three-legged stool:

- ➢ **Product quality**
- ➢ **Service levels**
- ➢ **Price**

Meaning, if I buy something, the product quality must be the BEST available, and I need it by "this" time. I need to get it by that specified time. It can't be five minutes late; it needs to be delivered by a time that is agreed upon. These two are the most critical parts of our requirements.

And then...we look at price. If you can't satisfy product quality and service, then the price is irrelevant.

If a restaurant chain that is buying AAA-quality tomatoes needs them by 7:00 am in the morning because they start prepping at 7:30 am for dinner or lunch, they need those there before they start prepping, not after they start because that's a problem.

These requirements are the premise for how this business operates, whether they are a country club, a restaurant chain, etc. Their entire methodology is based on what processes they use for preparing meals.

But that's a situation of fulfilling the client's requirements. If they need AAA tomatoes, don't send AA tomatoes. Don't send tomatoes that have been hanging around in a box for a week. Don't send the ones that were delivered yesterday. If they aren't firm enough, the restaurant can't cut them, and they aren't any good to use.

Therefore, we try to make sure that those two legs of the stool, quality and service levels, are taken care of first. And then we work on price, because lowest price doesn't matter if you can't get the first two, right?

As you can see, the first obstacle to helping a company go from **Expense To Profit** *is to help them be aware that an issue problem exists. Second, what impact will fixing it have on your business, and finally, how important would solving it be? This approach comes from my friend, Ian Altman, and his "Same Side Selling" book. Being open to solutions is critical to increasing the bottom line.*

Once that awareness is established, the **first step** *is to find out where the bucket may be leaking.*

There's an entire process that we go through with clients to discover this, and that's what the next chapter is about.

CHAPTER 2

Where is The Bucket Leaking?

Many companies in the marketplace find themselves simply trying to get by, in other words, they are surviving and not thriving. Clients come to us because that's often where they have found themselves.

For any company to thrive, they need to either decrease expenses or increase sales—and ideally do both. To help our clients decrease costs and improve their cashflow, we do what's called a C.O.A.T. analysis.

A spend analysis is a process to audit and understand all of your business expenses.

The goal is to find opportunities to save money and prioritize where your dollars go.

Our spend analysis method involves getting cursory data from a client first. Then, we contact their vendors directly because we always find the source of truth is at the vendor level. Clients sometimes decide to put things in different categories when they're costing items out, so what they provide to us is not necessarily what we find to be totally accurate.

One perfect example is a client of ours who is a very large premium vanilla manufacturer. When I was speaking to the head of logistics, he was telling me they were spending about $580,000 a year on **shipping and distribution** costs.

When I looked at the finances, the data didn't verify that. The data we got from the vendor didn't come close to that either. They were spending closer to $1.3 million. In his mind, he was netting out the difference between what clients were paying for product shipped to them against what was out of pocket.

So, while they were spending over $500,000 out of pocket, they were really spending $1.3 million. This is why we always believe **the source of truth is from a vendor**. They're typically going to have more reliable data, so we get that information directly from them.

When looking at client purchases, we then analyze exactly what was purchased right down to the UPC code. When they bought a case of items, how many boxes were in the case, and verifying how many units are in a box? Once we get down to cost per unit, we know the exact price for each specific item.

Then we go through the process of determining whether or not we can have an intelligent conversation with the existing **vendor relationship by doing three things**:

> ➢ Maintain or increase the quality of product purchased.

> ➢ **Maintain or increase service levels.** Additionally, if the client mentions they are dissatisfied with the service levels they're getting, we bring that to the vendor's attention to be corrected before moving forward.

> ➢ **Focus on pricing.**

We always have the third part of the discussion last because we want to make sure we protect both quality and service levels BE-FORE we get to any negotiations about pricing with vendors of our clients.

Our objective is to *not* change vendors. It's much easier for us to do an implementation from a pricing standpoint and just change prices in the system. It's also faster than going through the steps to onboard a new supplier, which also necessitates making sure client-vendor personalities don't clash and that they're actually getting what was promised.

When you begin to develop a new relationship, there are always different issues that develop. No matter how good we are at what we do, something can always go wrong. You never want to have something go awry with a vendor, especially if they are new. That obviously doesn't start a connection off on positive footing.

As a result, we don't change the client's vendors very often because of our work. In fact, this is "why" those relationships are maintained more than 89% of the time. Whenever possible, it's the simpler solution.

That said, when the client finds out that they've been overcharged for many years for the products they're getting, sometimes they're agitated to the point where they want to make a vendor change. And if that's the case, then we go through the process of determining how best to move forward and make a switch.

That changeover could be sending out an RFx (Request for Information, Proposal, or Quote). Unfortunately, most municipalities and government entities still seem to prefer this outdated practice.

If we have to initiate a change of vendors, then it's a matter of our inviting service providers into the process with client approval. **Our preferred method is actually using a reverse auction.** We qualify each vendor that we request into the reverse auction based on criteria that the client sets.

We then proceed through the procedures of having a "live" reverse auction, which has vendors bidding against each other to actually win the business. In a reverse auction, as opposed to prices going up, prices are going down. We know when we have the top two bidders at less than a 1% price differentiate, that we have found **market price** for what's being delivered to the client.

We create an online auction, so vendors don't know who they are bidding against. However, they do see if they're no longer the lowest priced provider. For instance, Bidder A is now lowest price whereas Bidder B used to be the lowest price; they now have the option to come in and make an adjustment to their pricing.

Too many companies focus on pricing first, in my opinion, but notice I didn't mention it...until last.

Maintaining or improving product quality and service levels without interrupting existing relationships is critical.

If at all possible, you can save time by not onboarding a new vendor if you don't have to.

Let's review the C.O.A.T. Spend Analysis Method as described by the chart on page 25.

Here's how you can apply the SPECIFIC STEPS in YOUR business.

COLLECT

Collect all the information you can about what you're buying, how much it costs, who and how you're paying, and who and how it adds value to your organization. Start with accounting and move through your departments, offices, and other places where the money is spent. Get that information into a single place where you can begin to work with the data.

You will probably have to work with whoever manages your accounting information. Additionally, you need to work with your staff and department heads to be sure that you understand *how* each item you're paying for is used.

Take a systematic approach. Start with general overhead, such as office supplies or payroll processing, anything that applies evenly throughout the organization. Next, gather information by business

29

area or department. Be sure to note vendors and contract terms.

Your approach to organizing your data will depend on what kind of business you are in, and the specific structure you've built. A medical practice has a different type of supply chain than a hotel or restaurant. A product that is shipped through distributors will have a different expense structure than one that sells direct online. As you go, you may find there are better ways to structure your information.

It pays to get this information into a spreadsheet, database, or purpose-designed software package. That will ensure the work you're doing now is easily repeated and maintained. The more comprehensive and organized your analysis is on the front end, the more manageable it will be to maintain in the future. The result will be long-term confidence that your money is spent wisely.

ORGANIZE

This step is about ensuring that all the data you just collected is accurate and consistent. Some people refer to this as data cleansing.

First, make certain you have consistent data by **creating a structure for each expense**. It should include items like:

- Product or service type
- Provider
- Amount
- Frequency of payments and/or deliveries
- Terms of contract
- Primary user(s)

Check for any errors, omissions, or inconsistencies. Consult with the people using the services and materials to understand their value, quality of service, and more.

You'll THEN want to organize your spending in two ways:

> ➢ If you group purchases by vendor or provider, you may find opportunities for savings. Purchases made from related entities, such as IBM, IBM Corp., or Cognos should all be grouped together since they're all divisions, and technically one company.

> ➢ Categorize by type. You can come up with your own classification scheme or use one of several standards for categorizing goods and services. These standards may be especially helpful if your business is large or deals with a complex set of materials or services.

Once you have a complete set of data, and you're confident that it is accurate and consistent, you can start to assess and analyze.

ANALYZE and ASSESS

There are four factors to take into account. Label each item.

1. Unnecessary Expenses

As time goes by, some products or services may no longer be used or needed. Consult with your staff to identify these. Set priorities on each expense so that you know whether it is essential or a nice-to-have.

2. Duplicate or Overlapping Expenses

It is often the case that different groups within an organization will have chosen different vendors for similar services or materials. This is especially true if you have multiple locations, offices, or divisions. This can also be true of online services, office supplies, hospitality supplies or services, and many other items. Consider consolidating to one vendor and taking that opportunity to negotiate for favorable terms.

3. Efficiency

Are there products or materials where you are getting weekly shipments when monthly would do? Are you signed up for 20GB of data, but you really need 50GB and are charged an overage each month? Or vice versa? Considerable savings can be had by negotiating with the vendor.

4. Vendor Terms

Do you know the market rate for what you're getting? Are better terms available from your current vendor or a competitor?

Do you have large contracts that are expiring or equipment that will need replacing? Are you **leasing equipment or office space** that may be up for renewal soon?

TACKLE

You have now set yourself up to make very good decisions.

Go back and review those items where you may be able to consolidate, get better vendor terms, or change service levels. Scrub each contract. Make sure you know all the hidden costs and carve-outs in each contract. Make sure you know the best available rates for your products and services.

It is also important to understand internal sensitivities. Some divisions have important reasons why they use different vendors or tools. Cost may or may not always be the overriding factor. Make sure you understand any special circumstances before you finalize your recommendations.

Contract Review Guide

We have an advantage here, as we see hundreds of contracts and service agreements in nearly every category every year. We know where the tricky bits are, we know the standards and we know how to have the complex discussions with service providers, landlords, and vendors that can result in very big savings.

Hidden Costs in Contracts

A useful case study to share is regarding two of our clients, an insurance group and a law firm, who have offices in the same building. When we analyzed their costs, we saw discrepancies. We could see issues in items ranging from **shared space discrepancies** to **real estate tax issues** for both companies.

We then categorized and assessed, and that's when things became clear. Both tenants were being overcharged for a larger common area factor than architectural drawings showed, were being taxed when there was an exclusion for real estate taxes, and were being charged twice for **janitorial services**.

Once we identified and documented these issues, both tenants received reimbursements and rent credits from the landlord for the overpayments. The insurance group received $68,450 in reimbursement and a month of rent abatement. The law firm received a check for $128,000 and three months of rent.

More importantly, we **established a process for periodic review** of all of their expenses. Now they can review and reassess every year much more easily.

These two clients are terrific examples of how the C.O.A.T. analysis can produce returns for our clients. We have many more.

The Art of Negotiating

One of our clients is a country club. **Food** is a huge expense. One product item was in purchasing 10 cases of tomatoes three times a week. When we entered the picture, they had already negotiated a certain rate with this vendor.

We came in on their heels and negotiated an additional savings above what they already got, because we made it "sole source" and guaranteed the vendor they were going to get it on a **cost-plus price model**.

With volatile pricing with different types of products you're buying like in food, you have to do a cost-plus price model because through our contract that we had the vendor sign, we have the ability to come in and audit their purchases from that vendor to ensure that the cost-plus is adhered to.

Keep in mind, because we're doing a lot of contracts all the time, we know where pricing should be.

If we see something that we think doesn't look right, we look to renegotiate it.

That's why people hire us. Remember, you don't know what you don't know.

But we *do* know, because as a team we've done over 25,000 audits across many different businesses, across many different expense categories, and across many product categories. And we use that knowledge to effect positive change for our clients.

I mentioned our vanilla manufacturing client earlier, and here's more specifically what we did to help them.

This client imports premium vanilla beans sourced directly from one of the largest producers, Madagascar. The beans are transported by ship and then by rail and truck to their processing facility just northwest of Chicago.

The beans are then processed specifically to a client's order and shipped out. Their end users are other spice companies, names you would recognize, that make chocolate, and other sundries. These products ship all over the country.

However, that said, 80% of their shipments go in five lanes—meaning, the top clients' five zip codes. We looked at their **shipping expense** and it was almost $1.3 million.

Their head of logistics, Dave, told me they only spend $580,000. I'm like, "Yeah, something's not right.

I asked, "So tell me Dave, what's your daily process like? How do you determine which shipper you're going to use? Are you using one broker, multiple brokers?" He said, "José is our shipping clerk who's in charge of getting pricing and scheduling pickups. He gets on the phone and makes multiple calls to different brokers to determine the best price that day."

I didn't think that sounded very logical even though he got the task done, so I asked him, "How much of his day is spent on this?

He said, "Between making the phone calls and then gathering data and making the decision, probably a bit over five hours. Marc, I'm not sure you're going to be able to help us. We get the best pricing every day."

And I replied, "Dave, you're probably right, but management wants us to look at it. Let's see through another set of lenses if there's maybe a different way that we can do this to effect some positive results."

Dave wanting to be a team player said, "Sure, great."

We contacted three of the brokers that they dealt with for most of their business, and we had them compete against each other on price using the same trucking companies that Dave's company already use. We weren't changing their logistics providers.

Then we took that data and when everything was all said and done, instead of their spending $580,000 net or in actuality $1.3 million gross, they're *now* going to spend about $780,000 before reimbursements from their customers.

Not only did we reduce the cost by a half a million dollars by going to only one broker, we also computerized it. So, if it's going to a specific customer in a certain zip code, you just send a pick-up to the agent. It's an automated system we set in place for them.

José was moved to a different part of the business, where they could use his talents better.

Instead of spending 5.5 hours a day, they now spend 30 minutes. In addition, they no longer had to spend rush fees because they could plan out their deliveries ahead, which resulted in not paying extra charges, thereby saving more money.

Now his broker who won the bid can cut his pricing because he is earning all of this client's business and not just a piece of it.

Same service levels, same trucks, same deliveries. None of that changed. All we did was get one broker involved, computerized the system, and saved them a half a million dollars.

The best part about this is instead of being $580,000 a year out of pocket, they actually had a net revenue stream. So not only did they save on costs, they also had about $130,000 coming back in *additional* reimbursements because they still charge the client for the shipping FOB at their dock. If the client prefers to pick it up, they can still come and do so.

Now let's go back to the other example I mentioned earlier, which was a country club.

We were already doing payroll and health insurance (I'll come back to that later in this chapter).

We have a great relationship with the club manager, who later hired a chef who thought of himself as a master negotiator.

Our team made a presentation to the chef, who replied, "I just negotiated some contracts. If you can do better than I did, have at it." We looked at what he just did and went back to the **produce** company I mentioned previously and inquired, "Okay, you're the sole source now. You're now on a **cost-plus pricing model**, what does your margin need to be when delivering nothing less than AAA product quality?"

He said, "Well, if I'm the sole source and I've got no spoilage, my margin needs to be 12%. That meant he needed cost plus 12% on every order. We recalculated what the savings for the client would be, to save them with only 10.2% above the contract they already had negotiated with this vendor. He no longer had the risk of spoilage, and he was sole source so now he's going to get all the business from a produce standpoint.

That was one piece.

And then we did the **non-center of the plate**. When I say "non-center of the plate," we're not reviewing purchases of steaks, lobster, or fish. We're just talking about commodity items such as sugar, silverware, plates, cups, etc. No one cares where you buy these commodities, you just want the best price and to be delivered in a timely manner.

We had a conversation with a large food supplier/distributor— that's who they had chosen to go with. The contract hadn't been signed yet. We looked at the contract and after a conversation with them, they were willing to drop the prices by an additional 8%—that's above the 12% discount they already gave them to get the business from their previous provider.

We told them that's a good start, but they would have to sharpen their pencils because we know there's still about another 10% there that they can afford to not charge the country club. They said, "I'm not sure that's the case," and there was a lot of back and forth.

After a while, when we told them we would put it out for bid, they offered to up their bid to a reduction of 12%. We then went to market: one company, of course, was that provider; another was their previous supplier who lost the original contract; and the other was a new bidder who was a local company and is always competitive.

Using the baseline pricing from the new contract negotiated, the new bidder actually came in at an additional 22.8% savings. The prior provider came in at about 16% savings. And lo and behold, the current provider came up to a total of 18% savings.

The new contract had not been signed yet; they had just negotiated but were planning on moving forward with the new replacement provider. Keep in mind these are additional savings above the 12% that the chef already had negotiated.

Now we're talking about over 30% savings of what they were paying before.

We presented this to the chef, and he just shook his head and asked, "I don't get it. How do you do that?" And I said "Well, it's pretty simple."

While you think you know what a pack of sugar should cost, we know what we spent on that item for other clients.

We already have relationships with a lot of these vendors, so we can go back to them and say, "Okay vendor, we need this pricing because you *already* gave it to us. We already know what it is." That's why we know where it's supposed to be.

When you have all this pricing data, you know what you should know, as opposed to being in the state of you don't know what you don't know. As a result, we were able to effect very positive savings there.

The same thing is true when we deal with an organization's **health insurance.**

Our client, the country club, was looking at an increase of 7%, which is not terrible in today's health care market. But when we looked at their claims history and we had a dialogue with their existing provider, all of a sudden there was no increase.

Usually, that signals there is more here than meets the eye. In this situation, we found out that because of the low-claims history, the carrier was making about 38% on their bottom line on the premiums they were charging the country club.

We then went back to them as the existing provider, and no increase was the best they were willing to do until we said, "Well, then we're just going to go to the marketplace and bid this out."

That provider responded, "Well, let us look again…" Now we get them to a 7% decrease. We went from a 7% increase to a 7% decrease. We told them, "Sorry, that's just not enough, we're going to go to the market."

We went to the market with another provider that worked out even better: better coverage, lower costs to the employees, less out of pocket—and it saved the country club 18% in overall premiums.

Oftentimes, as an employer you're paying 100% percent for the employee's coverage as an incentive benefit to retain them.

40

If the employee wanted additional coverage for children and spouse, you would pay whatever the initial premium is. But that was severely discounted to the actual cost. If you were paying $1,000 for a family, maybe they were only paying $250 out of pocket.

All that said, it was a great savings, and the country club was very happy.

*These two case studies are among MANY where we successfully used the **C.O.A.T. spend analysis model** to save clients significant sums of money on the things they were already spending money on **with the same vendors they were already using**.*

Trying to negotiate these deals yourself takes a lot of time, and no matter how good of a negotiator you are, having the relationships in place that we do makes a huge difference in the results we obtain for our clients.

In the next few chapters, we will break down how we reduce outgoing funds in specific expense categories.

CHAPTER 3

Protect Your Employees and Your Business

In a previous chapter, I talked about a client who we were able to save $150,000 on their health insurance plans for their employees while keeping the same coverage.

INSURANCE is one of the largest expenses in any company's budget, so achieving significant savings in this category can free up a lot of money for other uses.

While health insurance is essential to look at, there are many other types of insurance that we examine with our clients, including:

- **Property and Casualty**
- **Liability**
- **Cyber**
- **Disability**
- **Workman's Compensation**
- **Life (Individual or Group)**

Before launching into a comprehensive explanation of how this works, let's revisit the electrical contractor example I mentioned before.

We analyzed how his company handled their insurance, and we discovered that they were paying for their **executives' life insurance plans.**

Huge mistake.

I told him to give the money to the executives to pay that policy outside the business.

Why?

Because it becomes taxable upon needing it when somebody has an "adverse mortality experience" as they would say in the insurance business; it's a fancy way of saying the client died.

That becomes a taxable event if the policy is inside the corporation. But if you personally buy the insurance and it's outside the corporation, it's tax-free to you.

Most people don't realize that. This move alone would save companies money upfront and a ton in taxes on the back end.

The company's chairman inquired, "And the beneficiary is the corporation?"

"Yes, it still is."

Fortunately, he hasn't needed to make a claim yet, so I told him to pay next year's premiums outside the business. Take a distribution to pay the premiums.

This is one of many examples I can share regarding how we save our clients a great deal of money specific to their insurance and benefit plans.

Let's look at workman's comp next.

Workman's Compensation

This is one category where we are exceptional at finding things. Close to 80% of workman's compensation claims are not properly closed out. So, what does that mean?

If you have an employee who has an injury on the job and puts in a claim for workman's compensation, funds are set aside, and the insurance company puts it into a claims fund for that occasion.

For instance, if you have a car accident on the job and you're injured, you go to a doctor and there's a prognosis. And based on that prognosis, the insurance company sets aside, we'll say $50,000, because they think that's what it's going to cost for that claim.

At this point, two things happen: first of all, you now have a claim against your policy. This will mean that with the "moderate" standard applied, which is the rate that the insurance companies calculate for workman's comp, the premium will increase because of that claim.

You may have been at 1.08 before, and maybe you're now at 1.12. This means that the next time you receive a premium notice, it's going to go up by roughly 4% because the increase between 1.08 and 1.12 is 4%.

Next, all the claims that come in that are related to that vehicle accident are for personal injury. Not for the vehicle part, because that's on the property-casualty side, and those claims have to be satisfied as well, separately.

From the outset, determine who is at fault. Was the employee at fault or did somebody else cause the accident? If someone else, now they've done a set aside for $50,000. They are going to subrogate — that's the process that's used to go against the "at fault" insurance company to recover the dollars that your insurance company pays out for a benefit claim.

Let's assume for a second that it's not the employee's fault, and instead, it was somebody else's fault. All dollars paid out will get reclaimed from the other insurance company—whether it's automobile insurance or liability insurance. The claim goes against the other insurance company unless it's over a million dollars, because that's typically the liability claim limit.

In this case, the $50,000 set aside is unnecessary because you're going to get all that money back. In addition to that, the increase in premium is not necessary because once again, the claim is not against your policy; the claim is against somebody else's.

Nevertheless, the insurance company does the set aside as if they're not going to get the subrogation claim awarded, and they increase the premium as if it's not going to happen as well.

As the owner of the policy, you are obligated to go back to the insurance company and **put in a claim to get the adjustment in premium**: the reduction and removal of that claim hold on your policy.

You would think that the insurance company would be obligated to make those adjustments for you. They are not. Therefore, our service looks at the claims history for your policies to see if those anomalies exist. We seek to find whether or not the claim was closed out correctly.

Supposing you had a $50,000 set aside, but maybe there was only $28,000 paid out, forgetting about the fact that there could be a subrogation.

You have a $22,000 pot of money that's sitting there, and after two years, they have to close out the claim. The insurance company didn't put that $22,000 back into your claim pool, and they didn't reduce your premium by the fact that it was only $28,000.

Our process is going through and getting all that adjusted money back. Our task is to get the claims premium adjusted back, remove the increase in underwriting premium, and bring your current rate down. This saves the client money going forward and recovering the money that was overpaid in the past.

The same thing happens when you have an automobile policy. If you have an accident with your vehicle where it was your fault, then your insurance company will pay all the claims for all parties involved. If it wasn't your fault, then the other party's insurance company will pay your insurance company for all claims involved.

And once again, if you're not at fault, your premiums should not be going up, even though you had an accident. There was no charge-off for the insurance company. They may have had to put some money out of pocket to get your situation resolved, but they're subrogating against the other insurance company.

Health Insurance

Health insurance is very interesting because there are programs today where you can self-insure with all four major networks— Aetna, Cigna, UHC, and Blue Cross—down to ten (10) employees. Think about that for a minute.

Let's say you have 100 employees and pay $1.2 million a year. We'll say $1,000 per employee a month.

We help our clients by first looking at their claims' history, which we can get if they have 100 employees. Unfortunately, plans under 100 employees cannot usually get the claims history. That's a critical piece of data collection because that's the basis by which we can determine if there are savings.

Next, we look at the increases in premiums over the last couple of years, and what the claims were over that same period. We look at critical information such as who was sick, what the illness was, and who was not ill.

Of course, many of the **details are considered protected information**, so it's essential to be careful with it. But that said, we don't need to know who it was. We're tracking the type of illness and/or disability, but without needing the name of the employee. In most cases, a business knows whether somebody had cancer. A company knows whether somebody came down with diabetes. A business knows whether someone had a heart attack.

Why?

These are life-changing events where somebody is out for some period of time, and if it's sick leave, they've got to know why they were ill.

So, somebody knows. It could be Human Resources or even a high-level member of the organization.

Once we have this information, **we collect enough data to calculate the profitability** of that policy for the insurance company over the existing employer.

The goal is to provide a much clearer determination of how much the insurer should be charging.

Let's take a country club, for example. There are two guys on the board, big insurance mavens. The right policy is in place. Or is it? A closer look is always warranted.

Keep in mind, a lot of the employees they have are blue collar. They're cutting lawns (it's a country club), they're waiters and waitresses, servers, bartenders, etc. They're not high-level executives, so that's the kind of employee base here.

Opportunity for injuries is higher because of the type of work they do, such as a slip in the kitchen, or injury on the golf course removing trees and branches, whatever it happens to be.

We look at workman's comp and the health insurance policy that are in place.

A review of workman's comp usually results in favor of the country club because things are never closed out right, as I discussed before.

We find the premiums that are being overcharged.

Regarding **healthcare**, we look at the history of costs and significant claims. Like with workman's comp, if there are any actual sicknesses or issues, the club manager will know. If the employees are having difficulty with their hospital bills, they may be asking for an advance, for example.

In this situation, we examined the country club's claims history and noticed they hadn't experienced a premium increase the previous year. That's a little unusual since insurance companies generally increase the premiums each year.

We wondered why this happened, and our immediate thought was that the insurance company must be profitable in this account.

Upon further review and analysis, we learned that there was a 38% difference between cost, expenses, and the paid premium.

The country club director asked, "Well, what does that mean?"

"It means that you overpaid your insurance by 38%, not including a profit margin. If you want to assume a normal profit margin of 5% or 10%, you overpaid by 25%, meaning there's $300,000 worth of savings potential here for you."

"Really?"

Our recommendation to our clients is to do a self-insured policy. They risk up to the same premium level, $1.2 million, they were paying before. Then, we buy what's called a reinsurance policy, which covers any claims above $1.2 million. This means that they're responsible for the $1.2 million, and their reinsurance policy will cover everything above that level.

Now, why would an insurance company do that?

They do it every day of the week because they calculate the risk, charge a premium based on the risk, and then take that from the cost. That's added to the cost of the insurance. Therefore, if the insurance costs the same, and now we have a reinsurance policy, we're at a 25% margin instead of a 38% margin.

As a plan holder, you can reduce your cost by $250,000 in this example, assuming no claims above what was in the past. The margin is in the charge for insurance plus claims plus other costs. This means about a third of the funds would be available for potential reductions going forward.

When we presented this to the board, the two brokers said, "Oh, we could have done that." And everybody looked over at them and wondered, "Really? Didn't you tell us that we had the best option for us?"

Could they have done it?

Maybe.

But when you are dealing with insurance reps, they are there to sell insurance. Expense reduction people think outside the box.

What's the best solution for this client? Is there something there that's available to them that they have or haven't considered? Or even if they did consider it, maybe at the time it wasn't an option, or they didn't understand it well enough.

We got the deal done for them, and they benefited; that's the critical part.

They were on one of the major insurance carriers, so we kept them on the same carrier.

Nobody had to change doctors, and they got to keep their exact plan.

The only difference was that they ended up saving $200,000 the following year—and they saved $350,000 a year after that. Then, they saved another $300,000 a year after that because they've been fortunate that they haven't had any significant claims.

Note, if one or more people had a cancer diagnosis or had a major heart attack, there would have been some significant claims — they would have blown through that $1.2 million that they had set aside.

However, when you **self-insure**, you have money set aside, and in this case, it was $1.2 million. When premiums are paid, the money sits in a pool. In the second year, you can then start to reduce your money paid in because you now have excess in your fund.

That's how it works, and we're finding it to be more common, even for smaller plans, because there are providers and plan options out there today. This option only used to be available for large plans, but it's now available for plans down to 10 employees.

Working on insurance reduction is interesting because I'm not an insurance broker, and I'm not licensed—nor do I want to be. I don't work on commission, so I don't have a vested interest in which provider I decide to use.

I'm here to get my clients the **BEST solutions** and the **MOST savings possible** without regard to which carrier they are using. I'm not beholden to anyone. I work with insurance brokers to do the work with us to execute the plan we come up with, and it's a team effort.

All things being equal, we prefer to keep our clients with their current carrier, and we usually can without disrupting or changing anything.

Insurance is a big category where we help our clients, but next, we'll talk about how we can help clients add value to their employees without breaking the bank, specifically through the use of benefit plans.

As you'll find out, many companies are spending far more than they need to. Is your company one of them?

Let's find out...

CHAPTER 4

Add Value for Your Employees Without Breaking The Bank

M any companies offer benefit plans to their employees as a value-add or as a means of increasing retention. Both reasons are valid.

But is it possible to provide the same or better benefits to your employees without increasing your spending?

Or, possibly even reducing your costs?

Health Insurance

In our own situation, everyone had always been an independent contractor. However, when we hired a new "employee" as classified by the IRS, we added a health plan for the company.

I went through this exercise of selecting a policy just to ensure what we were adding was beneficial to the individuals and a benefit to the company. Looking to the future, as we add more personnel, we want to make sure we are serving them the right way.

In choosing a plan, I go by the theory, "If I wouldn't use it, it's probably not something I should offer them, either." Therefore, we looked at both a silver plan and a gold plan from a provider.

Both plans have the same doctors available. They're both **PPO (Preferred Provider Organization)**, so the employee can decide and choose. The only difference between the options was a **deductible** for pharmaceuticals of $10 in the silver, and $5 in the gold.

The difference in **copay** was $25 if you visit your primary care physician versus $30. The dollar amount of the difference in the **shared cost** between the employee and the insurance company was not that significant, but the **premium** was 60% higher for the gold plan.

That's a considerable difference.

If we had an older population, we might have considered offering both options. But in this case, right now, we're just offering the silver plan in discussion with my insurance consultant who uses the same solution for his agency.

We're also doing a high deductible plan to utilize an **HSA, a Health Savings Account**, which will allow the employee to draft on that money as needed to cover the difference in medical costs.

To offset the higher deductible in the silver plan, our company is contributing to the HSA, since both the business and the employee can contribute to this account.

In doing so, you can offer an employee one of the best benefits. The company can contribute on an as-needed basis up to the maximum that's allowed annually.

These are contributions the employee puts in pre-tax, so it grows tax-free, and can also be invested if your HSA provider offers that option.

Assuming over time the employee has a credit balance, you can withdraw it out at some point as a benefit. So, you're not taxed on the money you pull out as long as it's used for medical expenses.

Think about a 401k where you pay pre-tax dollars. You invest, you save, it grows. When you take it out, it's taxable.

Not with the Health Savings Account. It's funded with pre-tax dollars, so you're not paying tax on the money that's going in. Also, the growth of the dollars is not taxable. And when you do take it out, instead of like a retirement plan or an IRA, it's not taxable as long as it's used to pay for out-of-pocket insurance premiums or expenditures.

If you end up not needing the money for qualified medical expenses for you and your dependents, the accrued funds are still yours. It's in your name.

In contrast, that's different from an **HRA, a Health Reimbursement Arrangement**, that a business owns where the company can put money into it and then pay for medical expenses. It's deductible to the company, but it's not deductible to the individual because the individual doesn't contribute. That money stays as an asset of the company, not as an asset of the beneficiary or the employee in this circumstance.

As we were looking at options, we wanted to do something that truly benefited the employee. As a result, we went with the HSA for the benefit plan and we're paying 100% of the employee costs. This is another important aspect to consider.

Some say, "Well, you should have an employee contribute at least something because then, it's not like they're getting something for nothing. Otherwise, employees will incur unnecessary medical costs because it's not their dime." I don't subscribe to that theory.

I believe that if you need healthcare for whatever reason, whether you pay $25 a month or $50 a month or zero, that's not going to be significantly different. You're going to use it based on what your *actual needs* are.

And hopefully, you educate your employees enough to understand how to use a health benefit plan properly.

That's part of the process we provide, as well, in helping companies evaluate plans that best fit THEIR staff.

Benefit Plans

There are a variety of solutions you can offer employees on the benefits side that are cost-efficient.

Employee education programs, legal programs, and advisor programs are very inexpensive to offer. There are also combined programs where these different benefits are bundled together.

When you're looking at these options, understand what is necessary to attract the type of employee you *want* to have in your business. If it's a younger millennial, their needs are different than an older employee who might be 10 or 15 years away from retirement.

**Demographics will drive
what you're offering as benefits.**

There could be **voluntary benefits** and even additional **disability type benefits**. For example, Allstate and Aflac provide these programs where they pay you if you get a specific illness.

There is a program where they pay for you to get your colonoscopy. The provider sees the value of encouraging preventive health measures. Most only need this particular procedure every so often, so obviously that type of insurance is not always necessary. However, with precancerous polyps, it's recommended annually. The policy feature in both scenarios would be greatly governed by demographics.

There are any number of ideas and solutions available. Some companies give employees educational reimbursement.

The benefits YOU choose are dictated by:

- How big you are.

- What you can afford.

- What the marketplace dictates.

Depending on the industry you're in, that marketplace may dictate certain types of benefits must be provided to every employee. So, you have to look closely and know your marketplace, and then, of course, correctly price those costs.

Depending on who you choose, the cost can vary a great deal. An insurance company as a provider of a retirement plan, for example, may increase your expenses as high as 2.5% or 3%.

But if you went directly to a **mutual fund** company, like Vanguard, those internal costs are less than 1%. Note, I am not recommending Vanguard, just illustrating the differences with potentially a huge distinction.

Everybody has competitive products, or you can use an **ETF, Exchange Traded Fund**, as well. Similar to mutual funds, ETFs are a basket of securities such as stocks, bonds, and other assets, which are bought and sold on the open stock market. A unique advantage is that it allows for more agility to monitor and respond to the market in almost real time. Authorized participants (aka employees) can start to buy shares in the ETF. Today, you can buy these without commission.

The above options are all very inexpensive, with incremental percentage points over time that can be rather substantial in fee savings, if you're putting dollars into a retirement plan.

That could be the difference between your having another $100,000 in your account after 20 years.

You need to pay attention because you can't just put out a solution and say, "I've done my job." You need to look at what the overall, detailed internal costs are to the company and employees. Markets and situations change, so monitoring and having a scheduled review are essential steps to the successful administration of your benefits program.

We'll often get involved, like we recently did with one of our government contractor clients, where we've reduced their workman's compensation costs. In that review, we've also lowered their health benefit costs and reduced their retirement plan costs.

Their **retirement plan** cost to the employee is now 50% of what it was before. Over time, that's huge. We took 87 basis points—that's seven-eighths of a percent—out of the cost of their retirement plan. And, by the way, they have the same investment options as they had before, just with a different provider.

Our goal is never to change providers if we don't have to, but if the provider says, "No, these are what our fees are," that's fine. We can always go to the market and assist in identifying a new provider for the client.

Time off can be another terrific benefit. A good friend of mine runs a fractional CFO business. They insist that every employee, depending on how long they've been with the company, take a tiered amount of time off every year.

For instance, if the employee has been with them for over a year, they take a paid week off and unplug. Unplugged means you have no access to your email or anything in the office. They shut it off. You don't have the opportunity to turn it back on until the day you come back to work. The science behind this is that well-rested employees will return with higher productivity.

If you've been there three years, you're getting two paid weeks off. You've been there five years? Not only do you get three weeks off, but they're all paid for by the company.

Paid vacation is a huge bonus that attracts *quality* people who want to work for you.

In the end, knowing what type of people best fits your company and satisfies the requirements that you need keeps your clients happy. Inviting the highest caliber employee can be aided by having an excellent health and benefits plan, with plans that don't have to break the bank!

*Navigating benefit choices is a key service we provide, but we also help clients put money in their pockets by assisting them to **reduce the costs of getting paid** by their customers.*

That's what we will discuss next.

CHAPTER 5

Merchant Fees: Lower Your Costs

One of the best moments any business owner experiences is getting paid for their hard work and expertise. Still, the method by which you accept a client's payment can make a difference to any company's bottom line.

Suppose your business does a considerable volume in terms of the number of transactions or the size of those transactions. In that case, the right method of accepting payment can potentially eat up a significant portion of the expected profit.

Helping people save money on their merchant service processing is another way to help businesses reduce their expenses to increase their profits.

A perfect illustration recently occurred when we reviewed a client statement. They're an online business that doesn't do a ton of business, so their fees are not huge. But we reviewed it anyhow because I thought there could be an opportunity for referrals from this business. After all, they are very active in the online space.

Even though they told me we weren't going to find any savings, we still found a 10% savings for them.

How did that happen?

It wasn't a huge dollar amount, but we discovered that they weren't paying attention to the fees they were paying.

Their contract says they're supposed to be paying "x," and yet they're spending "x+." **There are 842 different fee categories for MERCHANT FEES**, and this client was charged for items for which they shouldn't have been charged.

Merchant fees represent a category where a lot of businesses pay money and make money.

Many software programs used by most of these entrepreneurs are tied in with different **service providers** that charge a premium rate, meaning 3% plus for their services, including Stripe, Square, and other similar providers.

However, if you went through Authorize.net through your bank, you could probably get better rates. That's what we do.

Our corporate attorney sent me an invoice for services that we hadn't paid them yet. This would be the first payment for the new business.

I noticed that when I clicked the link to pay, he was taking me through Stripe. And I said to him, "Michael, you should have a second option when you do your billing so that you can make an ACH payment because that payment costs you zero out-of-pocket and Stripe costs you somewhere around 2.5% to 3%. Would you like me to make an ACH payment? If you would, here's our form, just fill in your information. I'm happy to pay it by ACH, so you get the full invoiced amount."

Now, he's a good friend in addition to being our corporate counsel. Number one, I'm educating him as a business owner by letting him know that he could accept my money in ways that didn't involve paying a fee. But he said, "I don't have time for that; it's not relevant whether I pay 2.5% or 3%."

So I posed the question, "If you bill $1 million a year, is that not relevant to make the extra half a percent yourself?"

"Good point."

"So, when you think about it, when you say 2.5% or 3%, it's not a big deal. But now you have $1 million in revenue, and 50 basis points is a lot of money. I mean, wouldn't you rather have that $5,000 in your pocket? I'd rather have it in mine."

Merchant services are a complex product because, as I mentioned before, there are 842 different fees they could charge. Where the negotiation piece comes in is understanding *how* it works. Is there a Visa or Mastercard fee? That fee is fixed, it doesn't change, it's the same all the time. There's an **interchange fee** on top of that, also a **fixed fee** that doesn't vary.

Then there are all of the ancillary fees on top of that. That's where you get your **ticket charge fees**, your **statement fees**, and your **affiliation fees**. These and other costs people like to charge if you don't know better, can add up.

From an expense reduction consultant standpoint, our goal is to look at ALL the different fees you pay and figure out if you should be paying them.

And by the way, if there are **rebates** due to you, are you getting those rebates? Many don't realize you're entitled to a rebate based on certain cards that are put through the system.

Is there a way to know that?

Nope, not unless you do what we do.

My analyst who does the merchant card fee reviews knows it right away because this is what he does. He'll look at a statement, "That's wrong, that's wrong, that's wrong. Here are the savings." This is what he does every day. All he does is merchant card fees, and he loves it.

When you're in a specific spend category, you've got to love what you do in that designated area. That's why I do not focus on a single spend category. We have created a "hub and spoke" consulting practice that allows us to review plenty of expense categories While I like doing each one of them, my goal is to find the maximum savings for clients.

In a conversation with a hospitality company, which has a hotel in California, a question came up about merchant fees. I said, "Let's take a look at them. But do me a favor, send me a current statement, but also send me a statement from December."

Now, why did I ask that?

Because December was before COVID-19, I wanted to see what something in their busy time would look like, and then what it looks like later when they were only 60% occupied.

We wanted to see if there was a difference and if the merchant services provider was jacking up the fees to offset its reduced revenue.

Sometimes that will happen, and you don't know it. We had to see if the vendor was putting additional fees on that they shouldn't be putting on. There are all types of different games that the merchant providers do to create additional revenue for themselves, and you're likely not seeing the fee(s). You don't get a bill for it. The merchant fees are deducted right from your checking account.

People aren't trained to look at the possible discrepancies, either. They just see a bunch of numbers and think, "Okay, this is what it is."

They simply don't know what they're looking for. There are so many different lines on their statements because of all the different types of cards. A lot of confusion exists over what a client is paying for.

Most people pay 3% plus from **American Express**, but I pay 2.85%. If you are a business accepting credit cards, you probably already know the "x% plus" means 3% of the transaction amount plus a set fee per transaction on top of it.

American Express, for instance, is the most expensive card to accept. A lot of businesses won't take it for that very reason. Others may argue that it's easy and convenient to take, but why not take Visa or Mastercard if the fees are lower?

How many people do you know carry only one credit card and it's American Express? I don't know anyone like that. Most carry more than one, and if they have American Express, they have at least one or more other **Visa or Mastercard** accounts.

So, what cards do I have in my wallet? I have a branded personal credit card and a business card, both Visa.

Why? Because they give me hotel points. I also have a platinum branded American Express card that I use for business—for the same reason: it gives me points. I also have a Gold American Express card because it costs nothing in a year, for personal use, not business-related.

I also have an Apple Mastercard that I use a lot, which gives cashback. For every dollar I spend at Apple, I get 3% back, so those points can quickly add up.

A moment ago, I talked about how expensive it can be for a business to take American Express. Still, if you are an American Express cardholder, there are many benefits attached to it.

If you rent a car, use American Express because your American Express card covers anything that happens to that car that your insurance policy doesn't cover. This includes the deductible and lost revenue from the vehicle not being used while it's being repaired. The car rental companies will send you a bill for all that, but it is all covered if you use American Express. In addition, if I need emergency cash, I can walk into any American Express office around the world and instantly get $2,500 cash in U.S. dollars.

As you can imagine, merchant cards and merchant fees represent a fascinating area for us to take a look at, especially since it takes no time to do our analytics. It's effortless for us to figure out whether you're paying the right fees or the wrong fees. Typically, within a couple of days or no more than a week, I have an answer for you.

This begs the question: How are fees determined?

You might think that the more you process, the lower your rate should be. That's not necessarily true.

Your rate is commensurate with spend plus average ticket.

And believe it or not, the more considerable the ticket, the bigger the risk for a chargeback is. So, the rate may not be less, even though you have a more significant ticket dollar amount.

It's not based on the number of transactions, contrary to what might be assumed. The merchant service providers view this from a risk standpoint, not for an actual dollar amount standpoint. If you just have smaller tickets and have lots of them, you could get a better rate. But if you have higher ticket items and start experiencing chargebacks, that is a huge hit to your profile, and your rate could be a lot higher.

When I went directly to my bank, and the bank said, "Oh, the rate is 2.65%." I knew that wasn't a terrible rate because we were going to accept cards for a program that we were doing. My partners said, "That's the best rate you could get?"

I said, "Hold on guys, that's what they offered. I didn't tell you that's the rate we got. We got 2.15%."

"Well, that's better."

It's what we do for a living. We know what rate we *can* get based on our experience with these particular providers.

When we help our clients get better rates, 99.9% of the time, **we don't change vendors**. It's disruptive to do that, especially when there are multiple locations such as a conglomerate of medical offices, or even a country club with numerous departments where they are all using their device to process the transactions.

Because of all of the issues mentioned above, we don't want to change the vendor because we're able to affect pricing almost all of the time. Very rarely do we *ever* have to change a vendor. On those rare occasions where we make the switch, it's because the client is upset with their current provider for some reason.

Merchant Fees Vendor Checklist

When we do recommend a vendor change for our clients, what are some of **our GUIDELINES** we follow when searching for a new solution? This works for assessing a current vendor as well.

1. At the outset, we look for **whether or not the client is using Authorize.net.** That's the big network that everybody uses, and what we use to process credit card fees ourselves because it gets you the best rates.

2. Next, we look at the following: **Is the client PCI (Payment Credit Industry) compliant?** That's just a compliance piece to make sure you collect the right data to get the lowest rates.

3. If the client gets the customer's address, the CVV (Card Verification Value code typically on the back of the physical card), phone numbers, and other **personal data**, reduces your rate. If you submit that data with a credit card transaction, you get a lower rate.

4. If the credit **card is present during the transaction**, you'll have that information in the card, versus the card not present and having to get that information for lower transaction costs.

In many cases, our clients implement recurring charges for their customers with something already on file. In those cases, the physical card is not present. A card not present is a higher rate because there can be chargebacks. Besides, the client's business category can affect the fees a client pays for their processing. Specific categories tend to have higher instances of chargebacks; hence they pay a higher rate.

5. The least expensive transactions are a card present with a chip, and the chip is being used in the transaction. Those are always going to be the lowest-rate transactions for any kind of business.

6. With credit card processing, you have to work within a software system, and sometimes the software system is locked down with a specific vendor. If we are changing software vendors for a client, we make sure that they're vendor-neutral from a merchant processing standpoint because I want to be free to choose my **merchant processing vendor**. If they've already got one in place, and we're firing the software vendor, we don't want to change the merchant fees provider because that requires a lot more implementation issues.

IN REVIEW, there are TWO components to merchant fees:

- **PAYING money**
- **MAKING money**

We've already discussed the idea of companies paying money to have their credit card transactions processed.

How can you make money doing this?

There's a second piece to merchant cards, which is **Accounts Payable (AP)** processing. New revenue can be earned by a business implementing this feature. You might be thinking, *Wait a minute, but how does that tie into credit cards?*

It's because you're using either a Visa or a Mastercard debit card to pay a vendor. When you charge something onto a card, there's a fee to the merchant, while you can use a debit card program that actually will give you revenue back.

On a call with one of my municipal clients, we're working through this process. We took their accounts payable file, and determined that minimally, they can get $232,000 a year back in revenue share from the accounts payable process.

To do so, we're outsourcing the AP so they don't have to hire three people that they don't have the money for anyhow. The AP system uses secured logins for all their vendors eliminating the risk of improper information being registered or changed. So, the vendors can put their information in, and it all gets registered.

There will be an initial data dump from their ERP (Enterprise Resource Planning software) system into the AP system, but there won't be ACH information.

So, if it's a smaller local vendor, the client doesn't want them to have to use the debit card because that costs money to the vendor. They want them to be able to do an ACH, which means no more checks. We're saving them $5 a month per check they write by getting rid of checks. They process 2,600 payments a month, so that's a significant savings for them.

There are also programs where they can be paid fees using ACH as long as, once again, the vendor will agree to be in the program. It costs the vendor something, but it's not the same as doing a virtual debit card.

Virtual debit cards are a one-time use card. They're issued to make that one payment—boom, they're gone, they're done. It's all completed electronically today.

This is a merchant card fee "play" where you get revenue back to the business, municipality, or nonprofit that pays the bills.

We know this municipality will get a minimum of $232,000 that first year, and they'll end up with somewhere close to $450,000 to $500,000 the next year. Over time, it'll probably be closer to $1 million by the time we're enrolling everybody.

That's additional funds a municipality no longer has to find.

> **There is a lot of money to be recovered and money earned when a business sets up their merchant processing correctly.**
>
> If you would like to learn how this bucket is leaking in your business, my team and I would enjoy having a conversation with you to see if you are experiencing your best possible processing rate based on your transaction history.

We've been talking about saving money when you receive and spend money, but if your business needs funds more quickly, what are your best options for obtaining that money?

That's the subject of the next chapter.

CHAPTER 6

Strategic Ways to Access Funds for Your Business

Another category where businesses tend to spend more money than they should is **BANKING and CREDIT LINE FEES**. At some point, every business will have their money in a bank or will need access to credit in order to scale their company.

If you are running a very large company, it would be nearly impossible for you to catch where you have been overcharged without a trained eye to know what to look for.

Of course, that's why we're here.

We were in the middle of a significant **bank fee audit** for our largest client, who keeps an average daily balance of $113 million in their account, when an important discovery was made.

The bank they use for a holding account charges them $28,000 a month in excess out-of-pocket fees.

We did an analysis and found that the bank actually should be crediting them about $25,000 a month. So, we've got a swing from a $28,000 expense to a $25,000 credit. This is an overcharge of $53,000 per month.

How did we figure this out?

Fortunately, I have guys smarter than me on my team who work specifically in this space. One notably, does bank fee analysis and spent over 20 years with major, money center banks and a couple of regional banks.

He has access to the data of what it costs for each bank to do all transactions.

For example, he knows how to get the responses needed for these questions:

What does it cost to deposit cash, one check, or multiple checks at particular banks?

If the transaction is a bank wire, how much does it *cost* the bank to wire the money?

How much does it cost the bank to wire the money from bank to bank?

What do they charge the client?

As a result, our team has the actual cost data to then compare against what the client is paying for each expense line item.

On this client's statement, there are *42 different line items*. We found many places where their bank was charging 300% more than the bank's real cost. That's too much for bank fees!

In addition, we found they were not crediting the client at the **correct rate for the average daily balance**. With automation, the public thinks the formulas are infallible. But our experience is that the contracts and calculations require some scrutiny.

We provide the expertise to get those line items to a reasonable 100% above cost instead of 300%, which would save this client a substantial sum of money.

Their holding company has many subaccounts for the division's CFO, who reviewed our results. He asked us to talk to their bank and negotiate new fees based on our findings. The client is now enjoying an average savings of $53,000 per month.

We also reviewed the bank fees for another division of this client. The determination was that they were spending about $20,000 a month more than they should be paying.

We told them exactly what to submit to the bank. When they had their meeting, the bank said, "Well, you're right on some of these items, but here's where you're wrong." The adjustments that the bank approved would result in only $12,000 in savings.

The CFO came back to us, "This is what they said. They agreed to these items, but they didn't agree to this. They said we're wrong."

Keep in mind, we're not going to give a client advice on anything that we can't support. So, we provided them with the additional details needed for the two items that the bank denied. They went back to the bank and submitted the evidence—and the bank gave the client the other $8,000.

So, that effort resulted in $20,000 a month in savings.

Now, you may be wondering, "What if I don't feel confident enough to **negotiate with the bank** myself? If I prefer, can you do it for us?"

Of course, we are willing to handle it either way. In the case I just described, the client negotiated based on the results we found in their statement audits. In other situations, we do the negotiating for the client.

Like merchant fees, we don't change banks unless we have to because that can be a nightmare. Logistically, it's even worse than changing merchant fees providers. Keep in mind, all of a client's financial business is based on a specific bank. When you have new systems to implement but also need to change banks (i.e., requiring new accounts and source links), there's always something that can get messed up.

We worked with another client and completed a review of fees. We provided the CFO with the information needed, and he went to the bank. Although they weren't as large as the company cited previously, we told them they were overcharged by a whopping $36,000.

He came back from their meeting with an agreement to only a $9,000 reduction in fees. The bank told us, "You're wrong in your analysis." No surprise to us as we hear that often as the bank's first line of defense.

We provided the data to support our claim, had another meeting, and now they're up to $32,000 in savings.

The client asked me, "What should we do?" I said, "Well, we probably did enough for now. We'll get the other $4,000 next year."

So, that's what we did. We waited until the turn of the year and negotiated the rest of the fees at that time.

Every six months, they meet with the bank's relationship

manager because when you have many **loans, working capital lines of credit, and other expenses such as depository drop boxes**, there are always services the bank wants you to use but may have usurious fees. Their job is to try and sell as much as they can, so we keep an eye on that for our clients.

Bank fees are a mysterious unknown category to many because they don't know what should or shouldn't be charged.

For instance, depending on the bank's size, a **bank wire** costs anywhere between $1.50 and $6.00 with banks charging a lot more than that. I pay $15 for a bank wire, although my bank wanted $55.

I said, "No, I'll pay $15."

"Well, why would we let you do that?"

I replied, "Because I know it costs you $1.50 to do that bank wire." We understand how a major bank operates.

"How do you know that?"

"I'm in this business. I know what it costs you to do a bank wire. So, I'll give you another $13.50 because somebody has to get involved manually and their time is probably worth that much for the amount of effort. So, I'll pay you $15." My bank agreed.

People are just not aware of actual bank costs.

Some banks are **charging to deposit cash** these days. When someone tries to say that to me, I tell them, "Wait a minute, you're a Federal Reserve Bank, you can't charge me to deposit cash. That's against the Federal Reserve Bank rules."

"Oh, no worries, we won't charge you."

But they charge people if they don't know the rules, and many people don't question it.

We have the advantage as an expense reduction consultant.

We've done many thousands of audits on bank fees, and we have pricing information for all the banks, whether it's a major bank or a bank around the corner.

Having that information, which is not common knowledge for most consumers, whether it's bank fees, merchant fees, medical supplies, or whatever else, is an important part of our tool chest.

You're new to us? Where do we start?

Sometimes people ask where we start when on-boarding a first-time client because they don't always know *where* they are spend-ing too much money.

The question I like to ask to get the conversation started is my reliable opener,

"What check do you hate writing the most every month? Which bill can you not stand paying?"

One client, who spends $1.7 million with one individual

vendor every year, said, "The bill for this copy machine bothers me." He pays $3,500 a year for it, but it bothers him. Interesting!

I asked, "It's under $3,500, how can that bother you? You're spending $1.7 million with a single supplier, but you're spending $3,500 with this copy machine, and that's got you upset?"

He owned the machine and had a maintenance agreement, so it got fixed when it broke down or needed attention.

It's fascinating to discover what a client's hot buttons are.

The bottom line to all of this, especially if you have a large company: **chances are excellent you are overpaying on your bank fees**.

Just like the examples cited in this chapter, if you have no idea what a bank charges to provide their services, and how much of a markup they make, you have no idea if you are paying too much or not. We can help!

Another area where companies spend a lot of money is with their technology.

But are you paying too much for that, as well?

That's the subject of the next chapter.

CHAPTER 7

Maximize Your Technology and Increase Efficiency

Technology has taken a more significant role in how we operate our businesses and communicate with our prospects and customers. In larger companies, the monthly and annual spend in this category can be quite substantial.

The telecom space has evolved rapidly, not just from a technology perspective, but the pandemic caused a hard shift in how that technology is delivered since many companies now have more staff working remotely than ever before.

In more recent years, there have been scores of **conversions to VoIP**, which is Voice over Internet Protocol, versus traditional PBX systems. PBX is where you had a physical switch box in your business location with all of your phones hardwired to that switch box.

With the old way of setting up communications systems, this service was typically provided by a telecommunications company such as Verizon or AT&T. Or, perhaps by one of the providers of T1, T2, or T3 lines (the difference between each of these is in the capacity of the line). It also allowed for segmentation of how many of the lines would be used for data (e.g., one or more dedicated FAX lines) and how many for voice.

Today, it's a lot easier.

Most businesses have transferred to a non-PBX system. VoIP is plugging into a data line, just as if you were plugging your computer into the wall using a network cord.

The Voice over Internet Protocol has expanded so dramatically that you don't even need a plugged-in phone.

You can wirelessly connect to a service, and that service can be done as a SaaS service (Software as a Service), over the Internet. Plus, you can do it right on your mobile device.

As a personal illustration, I have my regular **mobile service** on its device and then I have my work-related service, which can be provided by the same company. If you don't have choices available in your area, you can use Microsoft Teams. I use this option with my voice provider delivering it over fiber, so it's an outstanding, high-quality service.

Based on your location, you may have multiple providers, but they're all providing data services to business these days using a fiber connection. You're buying based on the services that you need, rather than with a bundle package like you do with your home service.

There's a whole progression right now in business that would probably have taken five more years to get in place. But, the immediate needs in the market caused it to happen in five months because of the pandemic.

Businesses have embraced **telecommuting** (remote work), to enable employees to work from home.

However, when you're anywhere offsite, you've created a liability to the company in having access to their servers remotely.

How secure is that connection?

As a result of this evolution, **VPN (virtual private networks)** were created and had to be set up in corporations to ensure that communication over the Internet stayed protected.

People on these networks are using what's called SSL, or secured socket layer protocols, to encrypt data moving back and forth.

This means that even if somebody did hack into the provider's lines, your data would still be safe, and no one would be able to get at the information you were providing through the network.

If you asked me a year ago, "What do you think about this transition to voice over Internet protocol, and people having one device to be able to answer both business calls and mobile calls?" I would have said the process is constantly evolving.

During the COVID-19 crisis, the turn to VoIP evolved even faster due to a shift toward people working from home.

For instance, instead of using Microsoft Teams, I now can just have another chip in my phone. I have an **e-SIM and a physical SIM**. The two each ring separately but can call right into your mobile device, using it as a business phone, as well as a personal device.

Think about that.

You just cut your cost as a business in half because you don't have multiple devices. It's a lot less expensive to put an e-SIM in a phone, depending on how many lines you have.

Based on how big your organization is, we'll ascertain the cost per line, and whether it's direct through a provider, a secondary provider, or using a source provider like Microsoft, Google, Dialpad, or Ring.

There are plenty of services you can subscribe to in the corporate world today to provide phone service for business.

That said, what people are not keeping in mind is when someone calls a work number, they like to hear a friendly voice. Typically, if I'm not **answering my phone**, I have a physical person answering during regular business hours. Obviously after business hours, it's going to go to voicemail.

As you can probably imagine, voicemail is not an ideal option. That's because research shows that if you have a physical person answering your calls, 87% of the time, you will know who called you.

People prefer a live person to speak to rather than automated solutions.

Often, people will just hang up on voicemail. I get voicemail, and I don't bother to leave a message anymore. I just hang up. You can send a text, send an email, or call back later at some other point.

So as a professional person, if you're trying to make sure that you get all of your calls, you need to think through saving money regarding a) how you're receiving calls to your business AND b) the outward "appearance" from a public relations standpoint.

Who's answering your phone?

Are they answering your phone consistently?

Are they smiling when they answer?

Believe it or not, data shows that a person who answers the phone smiling can be felt on the other end.

When you think about that, you're not going to get a smiling face from somebody who's recording something. They may be smiling while they're recording it, but it's still not the same.

These are costs that need to be considered when saving money, but also ensuring you have the right system in place for your needs.

Our work with clients in this category involves BOTH telecom and wireless expense components because of the way technology has evolved.

Telecom Scrutiny

In our telecom work, when we complete audits on a company's phone bills—for example, with medical practices, big law firms, or legacy businesses that are passed from one generation to the next—we find numerous occurrences of what we call ghost lines.

What's a ghost line?

A ghost line is a line where there's no ring and no answer. You dial it, there's a number on the phone bill for it, but there's no answer when you dial it because it's no longer "in use." These lines were probably put in at some point for a reason, assuming it's not designated as an elevator line, fire-related, or a burglar system-related line (we also make sure we check those numbers).

On these lines where there will never be an answer, we know we have an issue when the client is being billed for something that doesn't exist in their in-house directory.

We're going to find out how long that client has been charged for the nonexistent numbers.

And by the way, if you make a phone call to the telecommunications provider, they can tell you how long there's been no activity on a line. They may not want to tell you, but they can. That's part of the research we do and when we do a recovery for clients with ghost lines.

So why do ghost lines even exist?

Because the client, or a prior building occupant, previously had a system where multiple lines were needed.

For example, if I had a desk phone PBX, that line wasn't shareable. This means that if I had a direct dial line to my desk as a traditional landline, it can only handle one call at a time. However, rollover lines (aka separate phone lines) may be needed so that as multiple calls come into a published, specific phone number, overlapping each other timewise, they are routed to a preset list of "available" not-in-use-at-the-moment lines.

I might have a secondary rollover line that nobody knew the

number (unpublished). The phone system could roll over to me so that I could answer that incoming call without going to voicemail or to a third-party answering service. It's far more personal for the public.

So, if the business has converted to a VoIP system, why do these ghost lines still exist?

Perhaps the business that initially set it up in that building doesn't exist anymore, and the current company hasn't converted to new technology. Or even if they have updated their systems, they didn't bother to do a proper cutover from one service to the other.

It happens all the time, and it's prevalent.

As a result, depending on the business's size, we frequently find a substantial amount of savings and recovery just by finding these ghost numbers. If you had 100 lines at one point, it's likely that perhaps 15 of them are ghost lines.

What's the economic impact of this?

The client is being billed every month for a line that nobody knew was there. It's generally about $20 per line per month plus taxes plus a 911 fee. When it's all said and done, that $20 line is about $27 per line per month.

Now we go back through the process and make a recovery because there have been taxes that shouldn't have paid for a line that's not being used, besides the recovery for the fees on those lines.

With today's current technology, you can also use VoIP with

your data, and you don't have to worry about dedicating so many lines to one type of service. The service will automatically assign as it needs.

It's that smart using fiber, plus the bandwidth is so much more expansive than it used to be. The system's software will automatically adjust as it needs more for data or more for telecom. In doing so, the cost has gone down dramatically.

I remember the first time we were looking at T1 lines for cost. These were from the Bell System, used as a communications transmission service with two twisted-pair copper wires to transmit and receive data or voice traffic. They were about $1,800 a month plus taxes. Then they lowered to about $1,000 a month about ten years ago.

T1 lines will cost you ten times for the same amount of service, and since they are copper and fiber, data speeds are denigrated. Every three feet, these lines drop in efficiency and you lose speed of service.

And because the speed denigrates so rapidly, you may not be getting the service rate you think you are paying for.

Today's cost of fiber lines is dramatically less because of competition, and the ability to access these lines is greater because of multiple providers.

If we see companies that still have T1 lines, we help them convert to fiber, of course. It doesn't matter who the carrier is; we'll save the client anywhere between 40%-80% per month.

Let's discuss a specific case study.

One of our current clients is an electric contracting company in the Chicago area, who has three T1 lines, paying close to $1,200 a month for each line. Do the math, and they are spending $3,600 a month on these lines.

They can probably use an alternative for about $500 a month and accomplish the same goals.

The other piece to this is that many companies keep phones and desks on hand for every person in the company whether they spend time in the office or not. Many phones and desks sit unused because they often belong to employees who are out in the field selling or fulfilling a job that has been purchased.

It's a colossal waste!

Why not give them ONE wireless phone with TWO chips to combine both their wireless phone and business phone?

When you transfer to this type of connection, it automatically goes to their wireless phone.

In many scenarios, this is an easy-to-implement option for those who work from home or who frequently travel for their employer. For me, whether I'm in my office OR offsite with clients OR in my home office, all I need is one device. It doesn't matter where I am, I'm getting all my calls.

With our electric contractor client that I referenced, during the audit process, I asked them, "Is there a specific reason you're using T1?" They said, "Well, we put them in a long time ago."

I asked, "15 years ago?" He said, "Oh, at least 15 years ago."

I said, "Wow!"

I then looked at the bills, and I *knew* we would be able to save them $2,000-$3,000 per month. And we did.

Wireless Considerations

When reviewing the wireless cost component for businesses, we sometimes find enormous savings opportunities.

For just one client, our team saved $186,000 a month. They have over 10,000 devices, and all 10,000 devices were on a worldwide plan.

We had asked, "How many of these employees travel worldwide?" They responded, "That's an interesting question."

It turns out that only 36 engage in all their travel. "How many total days per year do these 36 people travel out of the United States?"

As it turned out, one might be gone for three months, another for only ten days. But in actuality, they were paying for **international mobile service** when a vast majority of their employees did *not* travel abroad.

We provided them with an alternative service feature for anytime one of their employees traveled overseas. It is an automatic system whereby it recognizes their physical location has moved outside the U.S. when their country code changed. And as soon as it switched, it immediately turns on international service for that employee.

There's no fee to turn it on, there's no fee to turn it off. So, if they're away for three days, their phone service will be on for three days.

This meant the company was billed for international service ONLY PER employee PER day outside of the United States.

It saved them $186,000 a month by turning the service off and only activating it as needed.

If you think about it, they were paying an extra $18 a month times 10,000 devices, so that's a whopping $180,000 each month right there. Just by changing how the provider's features operated in making the overall phone service readily available *as needed*, this proactive measure made the outcome far more cost-efficient for the client.

We also found many other expense items where we addressed services they shouldn't have been paying for every month.

"Do you know you're paying for users to have a **subscription to premium services**? Like for sports and music, for example."

"No. Why would we be paying for that?"

"Well, they're subscribed to it. It's your phone bill at $5 a month. Do you guys have a policy in place that says if they want to do that, that's fine, but they're responsible for anything above and beyond the business-related app that they need?"

And they said, "No, we don't."

"Oh, so you need a template for a policy that you can put in place. We have one of those for you." We handed them a policy.

Their legal department reviewed it to make any adjustments because that's what legal departments do. But then, they DID put a policy in place. Basically, we turned off all of the extra services unless people wanted to put it on their credit card.

We can also recommend and arrange to have certain services blocked, if necessary.

For example, some people still call **411 for information**, which runs about $2.50 per call.

At the time we did this audit, it was still $1.50 per call. People can check the Internet and look up whatever they need, but if people are lazy, they call 411 because they aren't paying for it.

We had another client where we did a similar audit. It is a pipeline company on the West Coast that operates in three different states. They have a lot of devices in their organization, and in our original conversation with the CFO and the controller, the CFO said, "There's no reason for you guys to worry about our wireless program. We're fine."

I said, "I'll tell you what, just because you said that, I want you to send me the last three invoices for all three of your providers: T-Mobile, AT&T, and Verizon. Email me those bills that you can download by PDF from each website if you haven't already. Send it to me, and we'll just take a peek. It doesn't cost you anything to have us look at it."

He responded, "With our existing clients, our IT guy looks at the bills every six months and calls the business representative to make sure we're on the right plan and that we've got the correct pricing. So, we do these audits on an ongoing basis all the time."

Now, mind you, this client was spending $12,000 a month before we took a peek. Their IT guy made sure they were on the best options.

And I said to him, "Oh, by the way, we can save you a third."

"That's impossible."

"Okay. So, here's what I want to do. I'm going to give the analysis and recommendations to you and you can go to your business rep guy. Now, he won't be able to implement this, you'll have to come back to us, and we'll get it done for you. Even though we don't get paid, we're part of a partner network. And we are offered different pricing plans on the corporate side for the business rep that your IT person talks to."

They asked, "Why?"

"Because that's how they do business."

"So, you get programs that we can't get?"

"Yes, that's why I told you to send me the invoices. That's why you're going to save $4,000 a month."

He said, "I still don't believe it."

"I'm going to tell you right now; here are the five words your provider's business rep is going to tell your IT guy, "Those programs do not exist."

Write that down. "Those programs do not exist."

Sure enough, he sent everything to the business division rep and was promptly told, "Those programs do not exist." So, I started to laugh.

He said, "How did you know?"

"Well, I told you I've done this a couple of times before [tongue in cheek]. I know what the response will be because we're offered special deals as part of this partner network that they don't offer to anyone else. This is what we do for a living. The provider's guys are sales guys. I don't get paid any sales commissions, so I don't care what the price is."

And they said, "Oh, I think I get it now."

They now spend $8,000 a month instead of $12,000.

Then I said, "And oh, by the way, I could see about saving you more money if you wanted to put **all your devices with one provider**. It would be less than $6,000 a month instead of $8,000. But I don't want to move anything because I told you I wasn't going to. But if you decide you want to move to one provider, let me know, and we'll negotiate even a better deal for you."

He told me, "No, I think we're okay. We don't mind paying a little bit more not to upset the apple cart."

I said, "That's my thought. If $24,000 a year is not important to you, then just let it be this way. Your decision."

It's always a client's decision.

Whenever we do something for a client, it's always their decision what we do. Nothing is forced on them.

Bottom line, which is where it counts, we helped that pipeline company save quite a bit on their wireless.

That's how I have fun every day.

We find solutions. We think outside the box.

Since **data costs AND phone costs are usually packaged together** as one, we find tremendous amounts of savings for clients.

In this circumstance, the first thing I like to do when I walk into a business is say, "Show me where your server room is."

I go into **the server room** and quickly identify the different devices that are connected. It gives me a good idea of the type of services they have by the condition of that closet or that room.

Determining the amount of data that can be sent, are they using the right size Cat 6 cables and racks?

Is everything properly positioned in their switches?

Are they using 8-inch or 12-inch patch cords to connect from one to the other?

If it's double racked or triple racked, how clean does it look?

Then I ask whether they have an in-house IT department or do they source it out?

If I walk in and see different sizes of wires hanging all over the place, that's an IT company that needs to be fired.

Why?

Because if you can't keep your server area clean, and if everything is not labeled and marked correctly, how am I supposed to know that you're doing other things the right way?

> No matter what a client is doing for their data and wireless, there's an excellent chance we can save them a significant amount of money.

This is a category where businesses spend a lot, and probably more than necessary if they haven't had an audit or upgraded their technology in a while.

There are plenty of options out there for everybody.

It's a matter of knowing those options. The team I use has been doing this for over 25 years. When I present a situation to them and show where the client is versus where they need to be, they soon realize there can be savings of 5%-50% on what that business is currently doing.

I love the challenge of helping people be more successful and find money so they can redeploy to grow that business.

A Give-Back Challenge

An Expense To Profit policy we wholeheartedly embrace is supporting community projects and charitable entities.

Our practice is to give back 5% of the fees that we earn, to the community in the name of our client's business.

We give that back to a cause that's important to the company that we just helped, whether it's a community project, a social justice cause, or a non-profit charity.

Of course, we love when the business kicks in 5% as well and matches it. We want our clients to be able to flourish.

We're helping business owners put money in their pockets and food on the table, so that is an essential mission for us.

In the next chapter, we'll discuss how we can quickly help our clients lower operational overhead, specifically by reducing utilities and energy expenses.

CHAPTER 8

Lower Your Operational Overhead Easily

One of the biggest expenses a business encounters, especially if it's a large company, is with **UTILITIES and ENERGY**.

Of course, the first thing we do is examine how much a client is currently paying. The easiest scenario is if the client is in a deregulated market.

There are 23 U.S. states that are deregulated. Some states are fully deregulated, that is to say you can buy your supply, your gas, or your electric from any provider. Some states only deregulate gas; some are only electric. There are some states, like California, where you have to submit for an annual auction. And only if you use enough power, will you be allowed to even submit. And then if you do submit, there's no guarantee that you'll be accepted into that auction.

> This means that procurement is one situation where we CAN save clients money because **we're able to buy our clients power on a wholesale basis**—meaning, we're going direct to the power companies and buy it at no additional cost to the client.

We are the broker, basically, so **energy procurement** is a crucial way that we're able to help our clients.

Other solutions on the energy side include controls. A lot of older multi-family housing developments, for example, have a cooler for air conditioning and a boiler for heating. Depending on where you are and what part of the country, your **heating system** will be turned off, let's say on April 1 or May 1, and the **air conditioner** will be turned on. And then maybe September 30 or October 31, the air conditioning is turned off and the heating is turned back on.

All of this is not controlled by specific individual devices as is the case in most of the newer buildings today. Because of improving technology, there's the ability to now place centralized controls in the older buildings as a retrofit that can reduce your consumption of power by 30%.

In addition, there are also water flow controls that can be installed to reduce **water consumption.**

As a matter of fact, I was speaking to a friend in real estate who owns about 400 multi-family units in the Baltimore, Maryland area. He said, "Our water bills are killing us. Water is very expensive."

"I know. There are solutions for that. We can help you fix that problem."

Through some of the innovation solutions we have, centralized controls can be put in each unit. From an energy and a utility consumption standpoint, different states offer rebates that pay for the cost of some of this equipment because it reduces the demand on their overall system.

In reducing demand on their system, **local utilities are willing to help pay for better energy-efficient devices** because it saves them money going forward.

If you install these devices, you will save a third on your bills. It's a rather dramatic savings right from the get-go. Typically, the return on investment happens within six to eight months. That alone makes it worthwhile.

Sometimes we can even implement these measures without any out-of-pocket expense. There are financing programs available at the state level that provide no additional costs because these are offset by the rebates that you get from the utility company. This can usually be passed directly to the service provider that offered the energy reduction option, thereby creating another way to save money.

For those who are in newer buildings, there are savings that can be identified for you, as well. Some are specific to certain providers, which have you switch all your controls and meters to them to bundle for better overall pricing.

Or, there are other solutions that are agnostic, in that they don't care what breaker systems or what meter systems you have. They can hook up to everybody. These are open platform systems that deliver monitoring and energy reduction solutions.

One of our energy consultant partners was monitoring the energy consumption of a school, which was their client. At one point, all of a sudden, they saw a spike every night at 2:00 am, which was odd because it shouldn't be calling for air conditioning during the cooler nighttime temperatures. It just didn't make sense.

After seeing it happen multiple times, they discovered that there was an error in the computer code that was unfortunately telling the system to turn on at 2:00 am. Of course, totally unnecessary since no one was there at that hour.

Being able to find that type of error and fixing it can save any organization a lot of money over the course of time. Having new, updated technology can go a long way toward making that happen.

We have access to a variety of these solutions where we can help clients manage and monitor usage. Knowing we are on the lookout for even errors in computer code gives you the confidence that programs will run smoothly and efficiently to save YOU money.

Commercial/Industrial Expenses

An energy tariff rate is a rate that the utility is permitted to charge by state law, regulated by a state commission that reviews all filings the utilities try to pass along to provide service to the end user.

These **tariff rates are based on consumption and type of industry**. When we review bills for clients, we're always examining:

- First and foremost: whether or not we can help them with procurement.

- But also, is the correct tariff rate in effect?

Frequently, we determine our clients are not getting the best of what they are eligible for.

With my largest client, we reviewed some of their energy invoices and found on five properties that if they changed the tariffs, they would save a total of $750,000 a year in energy costs, assuming no increase in consumption. If they end up using more power than before, **then the savings would be even greater.**

We also examined if each building was classified properly by the energy provider. With the same client, we looked at one building they had in Texas, that actually should have been designated a manufacturing facility. This process involves going in and doing an energy study, which we handle.

What exactly is **an energy study?** We look at:

- How much energy a client uses.

- How energy efficient they are.

- What they use their energy for.

- And, if they are paying the correct rates.

And believe it or not, we actually count all the fixtures during this study.

Is that a T8 bulb? A T12 fluorescent bulb? Are there two of them, three of them, four of them? How many are in each fixture? What's the brand of the coffee pot? Is this in an office space? Is this in a manufacturing space? What type of equipment is there? What are the models, the usage, and how often do they run?

We do a complete energy study, which is quite comprehensive. As long as the building is considered 50.1% manufacturing from a usage standpoint, you then qualify to not have **sales tax** charged for your consumption.

We take a look at all the different appliances and devices in the building, including telephones, computers, heating units, and everything that's in that space, and where each is located.

If the phone is located in the manufacturing area, that's manufacturing. If the phone is located in a little office area, that's not manufacturing. That's important to know.

If the office is directly unrelated to the manufacturing, that's a different story.

A lot of facilities have combined spaces where they have both manufacturing and office functions going on, so that facility's operations are not necessarily 100% related to the manufacturing. That means we have to break all the data usage down for the energy study.

With respect to this particular client, although the facility we were reviewing was not classified as manufacturing, we knew it WAS, and we knew it would qualify. Our study revealed that they were actually 74% manufacturing. In establishing that basis, we were able to secure over $300,000 worth of sales taxes to be refunded they shouldn't have paid over the prior three years. All because of an incomplete classification.

This doesn't require changing providers. It's not that complicated.

It simply means that the building was categorized incorrectly with the service provider. It's as simple as that.

As crazy as that sounds, you would think a major international corporation would know and look for these types of expense line items. They actually do pay a company—not us, but another company—to manage their **energy process**.

The energy process is the procurement, the management of paying bills, and EVERYTHING that goes along with energy consumption.

The "other" guys just were not paying attention to this stuff. The details.

Our question then is why not? What are they doing?

In addition, we studied how much the company is paying for energy and found they weren't necessarily getting the best price.

That's part of what WE do.

There are different types of programs where companies might qualify. One, for example, is a **demand response program**. When there's a huge demand, such as a hot day in a specific area where the utility knows they're going to have an exceptional demand for air conditioning, they will allow you to be paid a fee to put your system on "off" automatically.

If you've got backup generators that qualify for their program (some do and some don't), then you can run on your own generator power while this other system is shut down, and they pay you a fee for that.

There are many other creative solutions. A major one at present is businesses designing policies to **be at a zero-carbon footprint**. A lot of big companies are doing this. In fact, Amazon has a large program where they're converting everything, and by 2025, they'll be at zero footprint.

We met with our largest client when they were talking about how they were going to be at a 50% carbon footprint by 2021. This was two years out from when that meeting took place. The guy who was talking about this was their vice president in charge of getting this company mandate implemented.

I asked, "So what programs do you have in place?" Because I knew of none, and we did a lot of research.

My philosophy is to never ask a question when you don't already know the answer.

He said, "Well, we've been examining a lot of choices."

I said, "So you're supposed to be at a 50% footprint in 24 months, you've got contracts that are longer than 24 months for power, and none of them are green power, they're all carbon power. How are you going to get there? Are you going to install solar and cancel all your energy contracts to get there?"

After our meeting, they determined that the timeframe is not going to be legitimately feasible. It's now been pushed out to 2024. So, we brought in different solutions for them. **There are solar panels that you can use that are bi-facial,** meaning it's on both sides.

They have white roofs on their buildings. With a white roof, the sun will reflect off of the one side of the panel, and the other side can then also generate power. You get about 125% to 140% additional power than a single facial solar panel.

There are a lot of **tax incentives** from both the federal and state governments to install solar because everybody's trying to lower overall consumption that is driven by all the extra devices that need power today.

Think about various devices people have now: iPads, tablets, computers, big screen TVs, phones. Everything requires power, and these incentives are designed to help lower overall energy consumption.

There are other examples, of course, of how we help clients save money in this operational overhead category.

We've done **procurement work** for medical practices that have multiple offices. One of these clients bought a couple of buildings and we put in place several solutions. The results are going to save them more than six figures annually with these alternatives.

As I mentioned, the return on investment for these types of problem solving is frequently less than a year. So, when you can execute these measures AND get your money back within eight or nine months, it just makes so much sense to put these new solutions in place, as well as a monitoring system thereafter.

We're doing a couple of projects for some hospitality companies where we're in the process of bringing them on board. We're going to look at their **energy spends**, recognizing they use also a lot of water.

There are several **water reduction programs** we can get them involved in. Instead of spending $1 million a year on water, we can get that reduced by 30% to 50% through reclamation.

We've also got a **healthcare linen and uniform business** that uses water like there's no tomorrow. They hadn't been able to have intelligent conversations with the utility on this one specific issue. There's a recycle system in place, although the utility refuses to allow them to discount their sewage for the water that's not going back in. They had no system in place to analyze or prove what exactly is not going back in.

We came to the rescue.

I've done this specific analysis before for other similar companies in the uniform and linen industry, where we actually go in and, for example, get specs from the manufacturer of a press. This type of business, of course, has a press for uniforms, one for shirts, another for pants, etc.

The specific manufacturer will tell you how many pounds of pressure per hour there is, based on steam. You have to convert that steam into gallons. Every machine is different, but let's just say that one machine may use 4.57 gallons per hour. Take that times eight hours a day, operating six days a week. The consumption for that one piece of equipment tells you how much water is not going back into the system. Multiply that out times 52 weeks.

For this client, 4.57 gallons x 8 hours x 6 days x 52 weeks = 11,407 gallons of consumption that's not going back into the sewer every year.

You can then go to the utility and get a discount.

We completed this analysis for a similar client. Their grandfather originally bought the business, which has now been around for about 80 years. The grandson is running it, so it's in the third generation. When the cleaning enterprise first started, the grandfather had a handshake agreement with the man who ran the water system to take a 10% reduction off the top of their bill, because he knew an undetermined amount of water was not going back into the sewers.

So, a new guy came in two years prior to our arrival, and he looked at the receivables and noticed that this one company, the linen and uniform company, was getting a 10% deduction from their bill every month. And, they've got this outstanding balance that just didn't go away. Naturally, the client hasn't paid it because of the gentlemen's agreement they had in place 80 years ago.

The head of the sewage department at the municipality sent them a cease and desist letter that said, "Pay 100% of your bill, or we're going to sue you. We'll forgive the parts you haven't paid in the past, but going forward, you can't take any deductions."

In one of my past lives, I actually spent time in the **dry cleaning business**. That's how I know a lot about this sector; fortunately, because it came to bear in this case, certain there was an injustice being brought upon my client.

After compiling the data and sharing the results, we had a meeting with the client and the municipality, which of course, brought their general counsel. The client also brought their attorney.

We sat in the client's conference room. I always make sure we don't go to the city's conference room; we go to the client. We make the city come to us. You never want to be in their territory because it gives them a sense of power they're not entitled to.

In the meeting, our client told the panel, "We've got a problem. For the past 28 months, you haven't allowed us to subtract the 10% that we've been deducting for 80 years. We did a study, and the study proves that your assessment of what we should be paying is not correct.

"So, I want to introduce you to Marc. He'll explain the study and how he came to our conclusions. We have a full presentation and a whole analysis that you can take with you when we're done. You can review it on your own."

I fired up my PowerPoint and launched into the presentation where we took them through the different pieces of equipment and how much water they use that gets evaporated into the air.

Then I put up the spreadsheet on the wall and said, "All of this consumption means that 14.7% of the water that's coming into the building is not going into your sewer system. You're not entitled to that 14.7% that you've been charging the client."

We're talking about a number that's over six figures annually. That means the overage is about $15,000 a month that they shouldn't have to pay.

They said, "Well, we'll have to verify these figures."

I told them, "Well, here are all of the data sources, I wouldn't give you something without a data source. Here are web links to the manufacturers that have all the information that I've put on paper for you, so you don't have to try and recalculate it. And don't worry, I didn't hide any of the formulas. The formulas are all there, so you can see them. It's all right there. Nothing hidden, everything is very transparent."

Then I summarized with the head of the sewer department, "Here's what we would like. For the last 28 months, you have not allowed them to deduct their fair share of what is not going into your sewer system. We want (and we laid out the dollar amount) 14.7% of every bill, which equates to $327,000 returned to the client.

In addition to that, by law, we're able to go back an additional 20 months—48 months total—so, we want that adjusted an additional 4.7% for those months as well." Remember, the client had already been deducting 10% from the bill, so the other 4.7%

represented the extra money they were entitled to.

That was another $80,000 dollars. The grand total was over $400,000.

He said, "Well, you know, I just can't write you a check for $400,000."

I said, "Right, you're going to have to go to the city council and have to get legislative approval. **And here's a draft of the legislation that you'll need to have.**"

We already had it written out for them to make it really easy.

"Oh, by the way, this comes from your counsel on other legislation that you've previously written to have approved. We want that done as soon as possible. In addition, we will not be paying 100% of the bill. We will be paying 85.3% going forward because this is an average of what we consume. We expect it to be the same. Any problems?"

The guy didn't know what to say.

So, if the city left things alone at 10%, this would have never happened. Now, it cost them an extra 4.7% annually going forward and back four years—the current year plus three more.

That's an example of how we help our clients.

I had another client where we were talking about workman's comp and he indicated that he also needed help with their water situation.

"Ah, tell us about it."

After he described the issue, I said, "I've done this before. I know exactly how to do this."

Clients will frequently think that we can't help them, but I tell them we have been doing this a long time and we've probably encountered their current situation before, or at least a variation of it.

Many high-end providers tend to use the same equipment. Perhaps they're using a different model number. Maybe the usage is a little bit different, but that issue is easy to work through. All I've got to do is change the equipment model. We get all those statistics directly from the manufacturer, so we know what numbers we're supposed to be working with.

Another great example is a phone call I got recently from a group that was looking to buy an office building, so they were wondering if we work with **commercial real estate projects**. They knew we work with commercial buildings, but somehow thought their situation might be a different story.

"Yes, we can help you, it depends on where you're buying and where it's located. We can help more if you buy it in certain areas versus other areas. But we can help."

He said, "How about **landscaping and snow removal?**"

I asked, "Well, how do you do it now? Do you have one vendor that does plowing and one that does landscaping?"

"Of course."

"No, you should have one company that does both. Why? Because if they have work during the wintertime AND summertime, it's going to cost you less overall. Although you're paying the provider more over the year, the bundled discount is passed back to you." You can typically save 15% on both services by combining them to one provider.

"Never looked at it that way."

"That's why you're hiring me."

We think outside the box, and that's what it's all about.

> As you can see, there are a variety of ways to save money on utilities and water, and there are many more programs I haven't even covered. They are constantly changing.

We've even had programs where we actually went into buildings and replaced all their incandescent and fluorescent bulbs with LEDs.

For a long time, the local utility, because they had so much money in the coffers since nobody had been doing any **LED conversions**, was offering 80% rebates to the client. Plus, if the project was done on a timely basis, they would pay the installing group, who had to be an approved vendor of the utility, another 10%.

So, 90% could be covered by **rebates** and we just wouldn't charge the client the other 10%. We would come in and do it for free. I can't tell you how many different buildings I did for nothing. I see it as a loss leader in that the client has the confidence to soon after utilizing our expense reduction expertise in other areas of their business.

Today, these rebates are down to about 60% total. That still leaves you with only 40% out-of-pocket. But, even at 40%, it makes a whole lot of sense to look at LED conversion because the consumption going forward goes down dramatically and the bulbs don't need to be changed so frequently.

You have to look at not only **energy consumption**, but what it costs you to have an engineer (i.e., **labor**) come and change light bulbs. And you've got to have a stock of light bulbs as opposed to a bulb lasting for 10 years.

There are a lot of components that go into the analytics. It's not just the consumption of the device, it's also the ongoing maintenance of the device. What happens if the ballast goes out and you've got to buy a new one? You've got to have the engineer come and spend an hour between getting a ballast, putting that new ballast in, and cleaning up after the job.

Do you need an engineer to spend an hour of their time during the day to change a ballast and a fixture? No. Put in an LED fixture and you don't have to worry about that at all. And if you need a new bulb within the 10-year warranty, they give you a replacement free.

For any advice or questions about this or anything else relating to your energy consumption, I'd be glad to have that conversation with you.

In the next chapter, we'll talk about an expense category that affects the medical industry, namely, expenses relating to medical and lab supplies.

CHAPTER 9

We Speak The Language: Medical and Lab Supplies

The medical and lab supply category is like having to know a new foreign language. The jargon they use is different from what we encounter in any other industry. That's why it's smart for us to partner with someone directly from this industry who speaks the specialized language fluently.

As you can imagine, just as in many other business sectors, we encounter resistance from potential clients who honestly believe they are already incorporating the best solutions. In many cases, we *know* we can help them—but they have to *want* help.

Our partner in **healthcare** has his own expense reduction group. At one time, he was the chief pricing officer and then the president of Cardinal Health, one of the biggest distributors of medical and lab supplies.

He serves as my **medical spend expert** and we collaborate to bring the best resources to our clients. I get him involved in every project meeting, whether it is a large group, a nursing home, or a hospital system. First, he speaks their language, and second, he knows the correct costs.

A critical part of the process in our analytics methodology is matching everything to a UPC code. If the UPC is on a box or a case of supplies, we need to know: how many items are in the box? How many boxes are in the case? We break everything down to the cost per item.

Many significant medical practices use GPOs (General Purchasing Organizations) because they think they're getting the best price quotes and lowest cost solutions.

We went into a large medical practice that had eight locations. They do quite a bit of business a year using a GPO. We examined their pricing and determined that there was probably $750,000 to $1 million in savings a year available for them if they worked with us.

And sure enough, we did our analytics. We brought in an alternative solution for them that would hit that target we quoted.

The practice did contract with us but chose not to change their existing provider because they claimed that they could save them about $548,000. Plus, if they made some other changes, they could get to about $750,000 a year in savings.

So why make a change?

The existing provider made it so difficult to make changes and kept changing the pricing all the time. Since we now are contracted to manage that every month, we're always sending their GPO messages saying, "Hey, you're not supposed to change pricing unless it's a countrywide manufacturer's price increase. That's part of your contract."

"We know that the price didn't change in Los Angeles, and it didn't change in Chicago, but you changed the price here in New

York State. That's not allowed. Our contract says you can't do it, so you owe the client a credit of "x" dollars." That's part of the process that we provide for our clients.

Our service delivers thorough analysis and expense reduction methods to implement the client's best pricing. We monitor the pricing to make sure that it stays constant over time. And if price increases are warranted, they're appropriate. If they're not justified, the client gets credited back the difference.

We track all of that.

The **medical category is particular and very technical**, and it's a challenging area to do expense reduction. It takes a unique knowledge base, and that's one reason we use a well-seasoned specialist anytime there are questions.

In working on a possible new project with a hospital system in Colorado, it's another situation to bring David, our specialist, into the consultation with them. The minute that happens, he and the guys running the hospital are speaking the same language. He demonstrates the high-level competency to offer data-driven, real life solutions. The intelligent approach is to ensure that I have engaged the right people on our team.

In any area where we don't have direct experience, **we bring in a solution partner with advanced skills in that specific expense category** with a profound amount of experience. Our clients know we assemble the best. David is a testament to that with well over 20 years' worth of applied knowledge and application.

He shared that in his previous position, "When I was giving a contract to a GPO, do you think I was giving them the best price Day 1 out of the box? No, of course not. Because I know they're going to negotiate with me. I've got to have 15% to 25% wiggle room on my price to make sure that when I gave them that bid, I know I've got room if I have to give space somewhere. But if they accepted the original offer, well, that's wonderful."

We use that knowledge base in how we get to market costs for our medical clients. And if we need to, we can always do reverse auctions to obtain bids to know you have the BEST pricing.

I like to lump together medical supplies and lab supplies because they cover similar areas of costs. For example, we can put in new lab equipment at no cost to the group as long as they agree to buy the supplies for that lab equipment's manufacturer/provider. It's a quid pro quo solution.

We're not going to overplay using this choice, however, as sometimes it's better to pay for the equipment and then pay a market price for the supplies on a competitive basis. You have to look at these different options when you present possible outcomes to a client.

We endeavor to secure the best of both worlds:

- The best equipment for the lowest price
- The best solution for supplies at the lowest price.

Thereby, never giving up on matters of quality or the service level.

> No matter what the expense category is, whether it's medical supplies, energy supplies, or office supplies, it's the same process. We're making sure that we get the correct quality and the proper service levels before we work on pricing.

As previously mentioned, the process involves a three-legged stool: the quality of the product, service levels needed, followed by price.

As a medical provider, if the quality of the product is not at a level that you need to offer the right solutions and services to your patients, and you can't get the product when you need it (a syringe, for example, where maybe you have a sensitive client who needs a three-millimeter needle instead of a five-millimeter needle), what good is getting lower pricing?

It's fascinating how the medical supply companies price their products. If I could tell you there was a specific formula methodology that they used, I would be lying to you.

The reason why I say that is because there is no methodology, there is no formula. As it was once said to me, "If we gave you a reasonable price, you wouldn't be able to negotiate."

And I said, "Well if you gave us a reasonable price because we know what reasonable is, I wouldn't need to negotiate. We wouldn't have to have this dance. And the client would be getting what's considered a market price, rather than a 'market price that you're *suggesting* to them is a market price.'"

It can be confusing when you're the end-user, and your supplier says, "Well, that's the best we can do." What are you going to do? Are you going to find another supplier for one item? No, of course not, you're going to say, "Okay, send it to me." You don't have an easy alternative. You need it. They've got it, you pay.

Our process is different.

It's different because **we look holistically at EVERYTHING**

you're buying. Typically, the top 20% of the items constitute 80% of your total spending. It's like the Pareto Principle, which states that 80% of the consequences come from 20% of the causes.

As a result, we don't concentrate initially on those other items you buy because those aren't going to move the needle in terms of your overall spending. Instead, we do look at the top 20% of the things you buy. That's precisely where we drill down to make sure you're getting prevailing market pricing.

Once we've had our conversations with the vendor to make sure you have market pricing, we can then implement a strategy that will provide substantial savings and will be worth the investment you made in us to find those savings for you.

Once we apply your savings, part of the contract we have with the vendors contains language that specifies no increases in prices unless a manufacturer increases their countrywide cost.

Meaning, if you're a practice on the East Coast and they raise prices on the West Coast, that's not going to affect you because you're not on the West Coast.

But if they raise the prices on the East Coast, but didn't raise them on the West Coast, that would affect you UNLESS you have the terminology in your contract like I just suggested: **no price increases unless it's countrywide.**

And because we do expense reduction across the country, we know the product costs nationwide. For us, then, it's not a surprise if a price gets raised but we can identify it if not appropriate.

So it shouldn't stun the manufacturer that we caught it. Usually, after the first couple of times they try this, they realize we are paying attention and they stop trying. Some just do it because that's how they do it, and they think they can without getting noticed.

We point out that this isn't the price that was promised.

We get the adjustment and the client gets the credit. We also verify those credits.

We make sure the client got the credit. How do we know? Because we're getting the data every month from the provider that says, "Here are the debits, here are the credits. Here's what you bought, and here's what we gave you credits for."

And, by the way, if the next month the pricing has not been adjusted, we have a talk with the vendor saying, "We brought this to your attention last month, you again didn't adjust it. Now, the client is owed two months of credit. Please get this corrected."

As I had mentioned earlier, it's incredible how people try to play different games. When you're not vigilant, maybe those games are successful. But when you have someone like us who is heedful of every detail, we find it during the monitoring phase using our analytics.

Maybe it was more difficult when you didn't have the types of tools we have today. Now, it is straightforward to pick up an anomaly on incorrect pricing.

Many companies are not observant of this, or perhaps they don't know what they *should* be looking for.

Remarkably, the larger the company, the more irregularities are missed, even though they are more likely to have a procurement team, a procurement person, or a vice president of purchasing.

They operate on benchmarks, which is typically an average price that people are paying for a specific item. If a company is paying below the benchmark, they think they are doing great.

But the real question is, "How far below the benchmark are you paying?" Typically, you should be 5+% below that benchmark.

Why?

Because when we look at things and negotiate with vendors, **we work on a cost-plus model.**

What does that mean?

Let's illustrate this with a case study. We were interviewing a large dental client of ours, who informed us they're at cost plus 15%.

I asked, "Can you give us a copy of your contract that defines cost?"

"No, it's a handshake; what do you mean a contract?"

"Okay, I guess that's one way to do business, you can do business by a handshake. What is your definition of the cost that the handshake was over?"

"Well, the cost!"

"Okay, I can give you about 42 different definitions of cost. Which one are they using?"

As I mentioned earlier in the chapter, my partner in this category is David. He told me he used to bury below the line of what they called cost to make up for all the concessions they had to make to win business. Fascinating concept, right?

They used to bury what they determined was cost—all the profit margin needed—because they had to reduce the price above cost to be competitive in the marketplace.

But that's not what cost is. Cost is what did you pay for an item? What are your margins?

Cost + Your Margins + Reasonable Profit = the Actual Price Paid. That's how WE define it.

We went back to the client and shared, "We've got results that we think can help you without changing any of your vendors. And, by the way, there's an 18% savings." The shock in his eyes was priceless.

"How could there be an 18% savings? We're cost plus 15%."

I said, "So, now are you cost minus 3%?"

He said, "Oh, you're really funny."

It's essential, then, to have some **definition of cost**. You can't just say "cost" because the price is made up of many items that are not necessarily cost.

We explained, "We calculate the cost *compared to* what you paid your vendor or supplier. With our supporting data, we can determine what are reasonable margins. What is a reasonable profit? Your vendor cost plus your margins plus a reasonable profit equals what you should be paying as a market price."

And it's incredible how countless businesses have no idea. Things are done on a handshake. The handshake is good when you "trust but verify," especially over time. I hear the same stories from clients who did not verify. It doesn't matter whether you're an electronics supplier, electrical engineering company, a manufacturer, a medical supply user, or a restaurant.

The minute I hear a similar rendition, I know we have an opportunity. Just like with our vanilla manufacturer, the head of logistics said, "We go to the market every day and get the best pricing."

"Really? So, you go to the market with maybe a $250 shipment or maybe a $500 or a $1,000 shipment, and you think you're getting the best pricing?"

"Yeah, you're getting the best pricing for that shipment that day."

"What if I combine everything?"

That's what we do: Combine everything to get a better offering based on volume.

When you take that entire spend over a more extended period of time instead of that day's shipping, you're able to negotiate better rates because you're offering to one broker multiple opportunities.

People we talk to may know how to **negotiate a volume discount**, but they don't know what the best market pricing should be. There's the difference.

The difference is I know I'm supposed to do this, but I don't know what my end game is. Where do I *need* to be? What *is* the market price?

Like I shared when we have two vendors competing for business and the difference is 1% apart on price, we know we found the current market price. I don't need to do any analysis after that. One vendor has the business; one wants the business. You're not going to make a vendor change for less than 1%. It makes no sense.

But what you HAVE done is brought that existing vendor into price compliance, so NOW you are at market price.

The other piece that's important in working with medical offices, hospitals, rehabilitation centers, assisted living centers, etc., is that **we are HIPAA compliant.**

Even though we don't deal with PHI (Patient Health Information), we might be privy to PHI from time to time in dealing with our clients. And because of that, we felt the need to become a HIPAA Privacy Rule compliant organization.

We went through the process of making sure that everybody underwent HIPAA compliance training and that we are certified and verified as a HIPAA compliant business.

What are the advantages of this?

It's a comfort for the medical industry client to know that should we discover something that's PHI, we are compelled to protect it and not divulge it.

Proper security is required to be in place. Even though we have cyber insurance and security measures, it gave us a good look at all the different processes and protections we had. It gave us a "dot your i's and cross your t's" approach from our organization's standpoint. This allows our clients to know that sharing data with us (whether it's medically related or not), has a higher level of safeguards involved in our back-office.

As you can see, working with clients in the medical and lab space can get complicated because there is a much higher level of trust and compliance involved. Having partners in the industry, such as David, who is very familiar with this specific industry's inner workings, has given us a huge advantage and allows us even greater ability to help our clients save money in this space.

Now that we've discussed various categories where a company explores saving money, let's tie it all together.

That's the subject of the next chapter.

CHAPTER 10

Tying It All Together, Implementing Empowering Strategies

I n an era where corporate budgets are getting leaner, companies look to trim back in various ways: staff layoffs, reassigning
personnel, cutting work hours, delaying needed upgrades, and
eliminating line items that in actuality sabotage growth.

However, the one area they don't typically look at is *the way*
they spend their money.

They usually *think* they're getting the best available prices on
insurance, telecom, and many of the other categories we've already
discussed.

I've been in the expense-reduction arena for a long, long time.
This means I have seen almost everything there is to be seen. If
you are curious about whether we can help you, we would love to
talk to you.

In determining if we are a good fit for your business, we look
at several key factors.

What does a good fit mean? It's not about whether we can
work well together. It's much more about whether or not the types
of solutions we can offer will make a measurable difference to your

bottom line so that your business can go forward in a positive direction.

After having done over 25,000 audits as a team, we've gotten pretty good at identifying *how* we can help out.

For example, we work with companies that have annual revenues of $10 million or higher. For those with $100 million, the savings are even greater.

Why?

Because **the higher the revenue, the more opportunities are readily present.** Even incremental percentage expense reductions translate to six figures because of the sheer volume. Considering that we negotiate with vendors based on volume spending, it just makes sense.

Determining the areas of opportunity comes down to several critical questions:

What issues are you dealing with?

Are those issues important enough to solve?

What impact will this have in making a difference for your business?

Let's look at the first question. What is the **ISSUE** that you're having as a client?

Most of the time, the challenge is that companies don't have the cash flow necessary to grow their business.

Perhaps they aren't able to replace a piece of equipment for a needed upgrade. They may need to hire somebody on their sales team or participate in a growth opportunity. Or, perhaps they want to introduce brand-new in-house training.

Most companies believe that they're paying the right prices. Our job is to show them that what they're actually paying may not be the best price and prove it.

I asked my electrical contractor client why he was purchasing from Vendor A when Vendor B does the same thing? It turns out they had an 83-year relationship he wanted to honor, and he was convinced that he was getting the best price based on the longevity of the relationship. Unfortunately, over time, he was not. Markets and supplies change annually and need to be routinely reviewed.

This scenario is very similar to what we find in every situation we examine. I always get the same answers.

So, identifying the issue is essential, and so is knowing what problem we are solving. If there isn't any matter for us to resolve, then there's no reason to hire us.

The second question relates to **IMPORTANCE**. How important is it to solve that issue? If it's not vital, then it's not one that needs to be remedied. But if it is valuable, then what **IMPACT** is it going to have on your business?

In defining the issue, we can determine how important it is to fix it, find its solution, and then impact the client's bottom line.

That impact typically comes down to one of two things:

➢ Finding the cash flow necessary to grow your business to get it to the next level.

➢ Helping a business owner who, "Hasn't taken a paycheck in six months."

We find the second response to be a frequent response in smaller businesses.

We observe business owners paying their employees and not taking any money themselves because they feel responsible for ensuring that their employees remain employed. This problem became even more magnified during the COVID-19 closures.

The owner's priority is to maintain their business with the thinking that at some point, revenue will come back, so they'll be able to restart taking income.

When we can identify the areas where a company is overpaying, it frees up cash flow. Clients can then do everything they need to do to stay afloat and even invest in their businesses. This focus is having a major impact on many businesses we are helping right now.

WHAT we do and HOW we do it are KEY in our ability to offload as much data research and analysis as possible from the business.

How? I'll tell a business owner, "I need five minutes of somebody's time for each category."

I know that in five minutes they can find an invoice, a contract, and share the contact information needed to speak to a vendor, supplier, or provider of a service in a prepared, intelligent conversation.

We're going to get all of the historical data concerning their spending, assuming we have determined there's an opportunity to save the company money in a given expense category.

We're not going to get that information from the client. As I mentioned early on, the vendor is the most accurate source of that information.

So, there's no need to create reports for our review—we only need:

- One invoice

- One contract or agreement, if applicable

- Contact information

The client signs a **letter of authorization**, which permits us to speak to the vendor on their behalf. It also informs the vendor that we are authorized to speak on behalf of the client, but have no authority to make any changes on the client's account. ANY changes have to be authorized by the client.

All of our work can be offsite, meaning that we don't have to visit the client in person. That enables us to work seamlessly nationwide.

Depending on the size of the client's business, the economic impact of the SAVINGS we find is typically:

- Significant
- Meaningful
- Helpful
- In the Six-Figure range.

Because of the value to be provided, clients want us to get to it right away.

As we progress, we remind the client that the initial process happens over the period of a year's time. As a part of the evaluation and implementation phases, we have 36-month agreements with our vendors. This ensures that the client has the advantage of experiencing the **savings AND our ongoing efforts** to achieve the best pricing available at any given time.

We get paid based on our success in securing savings for our clients. There's no risk to them.

We come in, do our analytics, and write detailed reports about our findings, to which they can say "yes" or "no" to working with us. That being said,

We find that we can help 99% of the companies we talk to simply because, "You don't know what you don't know."

This raises an interesting question. What if someone takes our report and tries to implement our findings without paying us?

Our agreement clearly states that we can review their expenses over the next five years to safeguard our work.

We believe in being paid for our work, just like everyone else does.

In our 30 years of service, we've only had one client that did not pay us the fees we were owed. That's because they sold the business, and the purchaser was not aware of the liability. In the end, we did eventually get paid.

THE ENDGAME

To summarize, our position is very straightforward.

> **We identify expenses to reduce or eliminate via our proprietary analytic systems, vendor network, and the power of negotiating. In doing so, we create greater profitability for our clients.**

Why?

According to Tony Hsieh, CEO of Zappos.com:

> "There is a transformative shift in business, and what worked before is no longer an option. It's time for evolved entrepreneurs, visionary creators, and change-makers to rewrite the rules of business for the 21st century."

According to Deloitte:

> "Purpose-driven companies witness higher market share gains and grow 3x faster on average than their competitors, all while achieving higher workforce and customer satisfaction."

The Expense To Profit Mission is to help businesses save money and improve their cash flow.

In addition, we want to improve the world around us by setting aside 5% of the fees we earn and donate it to a cause directed by our client. If our client supports a specific social cause or a non-profit in the community, we want to honor that by giving back part of what we earn.

How to benefit YOUR business?

Before reading this book, the idea of "expense reduction" being a certified consultant category might be a novel concept. I've shared a myriad of ideas and solutions to enable you to take a closer look at how your organization spends money. There are a number of to-do lists of how to get started in organizing your data.

Getting started is the clencher, right? From there, may I humbly offer the services of Expense To Profit to have us take an initial peek at what you may have overlooked. We've been able to establish a track record of satisfied clients, and the strength of our approach is that there is no fee unless we're successful.

Why Expense To Profit, specifically?

1. We can help just about every type of business out there.

    As a team, we've done over 25,000 audits. There's probably not a business sector we haven't examined. But, I look forward to the opportunity to get stumped!

    At a time when I thought that we had covered them all, I was introduced to a Boeing subcontractor who was stress testing airplane parts. My first thought was, "I've never helped anyone in that niche before."

    Our team is so diverse in their abilities and backgrounds that we *always* find a way to help...no matter the industry.

2. We have a process and a methodology of reducing expenses and buying right.

    Our expertise can be implemented across any industry: manufacturing, consulting, professional services organizations, non-profits, healthcare, or hospitality space.

    It doesn't matter if your business is vertical; our process is repeatable.

3. We learn something new every day.

    There are always innovative processes that come along to master something fresh and invaluable. With the most up-to-date tools, we are better equipped in how we address a client's challenges to spend less without sacrificing what it is they bring to the marketplace.

4. Our commitment to our clients comes back to the three-legged stool we discussed earlier:

- We seek the highest product quality.

- We then ensure the level of service you require and expect is in place.

- We concentrate on getting "market" pricing, after the first two legs are satisfied.

  If you don't have the first two, the third one will not help you succeed.

5. We really love what we do and thoroughly enjoy helping our clients! The examples and case studies I've included, plus testimonials provided, demonstrate we have garnered great reviews. These may have piqued your interest that we can very likely assist YOU, whatever your situation.

Creating empowering, value-add strategies...

Beyond the scope of this book, determining if we can be of help to you and your company is the next step. We realize that not everyone who we meet will hire us. It is my hope that this book highlights the reasons why you would engage our firm, how our strategies can improve your bottom line and why these methods work.

The suggested expense categories we've highlighted should be implemented as guidelines in your company. A systematic review of key vendor pricing will make a difference in tangible dollars. This closer scrutiny helps management gain a unique perspective in better assessing spending patterns and expense reduction.

Expectations and follow through with downline staff responsible for the expense is greatly improved.

There aren't enough pages to share the details and stories of how to completely do this on your own. THIS is where we come in.

So, let's connect to *continue* our conversation about how we can:

✓ Help YOU and your business thrive.

✓ Save money on that expense you hate writing a check for every month.

✓ Eliminate costs that sabotage your company's growth.

It doesn't cost anything to talk to us. Contact us to have a discussion to determine if we are a good FIT (Finding Impact Together). Challenge us to tackle your situation and see what results in expense reduction we'll uncover.

If you can improve your cash flow in tried and true methods like ours, you'll want to know more.

We share strategies that empower making prudent, informed choices and putting maintenance systems in place to keep the best pricing in line with your industry and market.

We are Expense Reduction Consultants. That's what we do every day for YOU.

I look forward to navigating this journey with you. Reach out to us at **www.expensetoprofit.com**.

QUICK REFERENCE: LEARNING POINTS

**You don't see a specific category of interest?
It's just not in this book...**

Contact us at: <u>www.expensetoprofit.com</u>

ACKNOWLEDGMENTS

A big thank you to Trevor Crane and the Epic Author team for helping me complete this book project. I can now check this off my to-do list for the past five years. His constant coaching and dedicated focus made this a reality. Thanks to Brian Wright, who helped get my thoughts and stories to paper. Ann Niemann's editing and formatting suggestions were brilliant. I credit her with significant improvements in organization, readability, and bringing clarity to my stories.

I want to thank my good friend Ian Altman. As I built my Expense Reduction practice, his reminders at our "business lunches" about ensuring you are providing value to your clients will be paramount to being successful. Also, he introduced me to Derek and Melanie Coburn, the creators of Cadre. Through the programs they create, I met with my "Un-networking Committee," especially Jeff Lesher and Heinan Landa. They always motivated me and provided great insight into getting this book titled and completed.

I want to give special thanks to my wife, Sheri. She has tremendous patience being an entrepreneur's spouse with all the business interruptions and meetings that pop up unannounced!

ABOUT THE AUTHOR

M arc Freedman is a Certified Expense Reduction Consultant and currently serves as our Chief Cost Evaluator, expertly advising our client management team on how to help you successfully achieve your business and financial growth goals. To all he consults with, he is a respected mentor. He is an avid collaborator and contributor to the spend consultant community, guiding thought leaders to formulate, design, and install the best operational solutions available to their clients.

As founder and CEO of Expense To Profit, he utilizes his 40 years of experience by efficiently implementing his comprehensive solutions to control client costs and focus on individual successes. With his guidance, over 89% of his clients have found no need to change their partners or vendors, enabling them to continue with their daily operations as usual. He would be thrilled to talk with you about how to improve your financial strategy.

Go to **www.expensetoprofit.com** to learn more.

Made in the USA
Middletown, DE
16 January 2021